FOCUSING CHANGE TO WIN

Leadership Change Manual

Kelly Nwosu   Nick Anderson

Focusing Change to Win
Copyright ©2014 by
New Catalyst Management Services Ltd.

ISBN-13: 978-1493653133
ISBN: 149365313X

- Library of Congress Control Number: 2014913043
- LCCN Imprint Name: CreateSpace Independent
  Publishing Platform
  North Charleston, South Carolina

Published in USA by
CreateSpace.

For further information contact
Official site: www.newcatalyst.net
Book site: www.focusingchangetowin.com
E-mail: info@newcatalyst.net

Contents

CHARTS

TABLES

ACTION POINTS

Acknowledgments

Kelly and Nick would like to acknowledge New Catalyst's editorial team.

These are the critical friends who believe in the importance of shedding more light on leading sustained, successful change. They also share our passion for making this book readable and accessible to contributors from many different countries. Their feedback is so valued by us as authors, who often can't see the forest for the trees.

Thank you!

- Dr. Ken Trzaska, Dean of Instruction, Gogebic College, Michigan; Terry Merriman, Managing Principal, PDS Group, LTD; Alan Headbloom, Founder, Headbloom Cross-cultural Communications; Diane Powell, retired teacher, Past President of PEO in Idaho; Jack Robinson, President at New Millennium Training and Development; Jacquelyn Wieland, Managing Director, Solutions Provided.

Reader's Guide

As people have different reading preferences, here is a guide to getting the best out of this book.

Sections

Each section organizes contributor comments in subsections with the author's commentary. At the end of each section, there is a section summary followed by action points.

Action Points

These are distilled contributor wisdom designed to help the reader review and enact a section's findings.

Questionnaires

At the end of sections 4–6, there are questionnaires to rate your organization's performance in terms of measuring change, thriving and surviving, and communicating change. Each is based on over seven hundred contributor comments. They are designed to engage those involved in change management and leadership to select those questions that are relevant to their change and then reach a consensus on improvement areas.

Charts

This is a snapshot of charts summarizing many of the survey's statistics.

Reader Feedback

Managing change in our times has never been more challenging. We recognize the body of work in change management is extensive, if not fragmented. It's too big to say that we have acknowledged all our predecessors or have all the answers.

We believe in a community of critical friends to deepen understanding and application of change management. So we welcome correction, insight, and collaboration.

Contact New Catalyst

To give feedback, arrange a speaking engagement, or discuss how we may help your organization, please contact us:

Book site: www.focusingchangetowin.com
Official site: www.newcatalyst.net
Email: info@newcatalyst.net
Phone: Kelly (+234)8159994865, Nick (+1) 616-745-8667

Thank you,
Nick Anderson and Kelly Nwosu

Foreword

In many of my keynote speeches and workshops on leading change, I start with this question: "What percentage of change initiatives creates a positive business value when they 'go live'"? Leaders yell out numbers such as 30 percent, 5 percent, and 50 percent. Then I say, "The answer is actually zero! Zero. It is zero because when any change— a large reorganization, a merger or acquisition, a new CEO or new executive—is put in place, the benefit isn't realized yet. The hard work begins *after* the change is implemented. It takes six to twenty-four months to sort out all the challenges. That is why your company hired you. If there weren't any change, we wouldn't need you: we could just hire managers. But we need people in the job called *leader* to lead the way through the uncertainty."

I have had the honor and privilege to help thousands of executives around the world navigate this uncertainty. After working closely with top executives in the midst of change, one thing is clear. The biggest barrier to success is figuring out how to deal with the people! Trust, motivation, job satisfaction, stress management, and entrepreneurial thinking are central to leading any team. But when you are motivating a team within a rapidly changing environment, these issues are magnified and multiplied.

This is why I am so impressed with the book *Focusing Change to Win*. It is one of the most extensive, detailed resource books I have seen for leaders. Whether you are looking for research on why people resist change, insight into how to measure change success, best practices for communicating change, or to compare what you are doing with what other organizations do, the answers are in here! *Focusing Change to Win* is jam-packed with information and practical tools for leaders to navigate the ins and outs of leading change.

Thank you, Kelly and Nick, for taking the time and energy to compile this manual. It is a great contribution to the field and will help leaders everywhere make change work.

—Lawrence Polsky, coauthor of *Rapid Retooling* and
Perfect Phrases for Communicating Change

Section 1: Introduction

1.1. Why Focusing Change to Win?

We started out with concerns about change management's poor track record. These concerns developed from our consulting experience, through to surveys from Kotter in 1996 to McKinsey in 2009[1]. All these sources show no improvement in the proportion of successful change initiatives. The primary reason for such poor results, according to those surveyed, was, and still is, people.

Our consulting projects told us that one likely reason is that people are unclear, even unaware, on what is expected of them. Our experience also showed that executives do not understand what people expect in return. For example, our own projects continue to show that 70 percent or more of leaders' expectations are not known to those implementing their changes.

Now, fifteen years on, economic turbulence and failed change are not making change management any easier. Yet some organizations do manage successful change. This puzzle is what motivated this book and led to this question:

About This Survey

- Mar–Dec 2011
- 1072 leaders, owners, managers, and change professionals
- 510 C-level contributors
- 58 percent outside USA from eightyCountries
- 19 industry sectors
- $10 Million to $5 Billion annual revenues
- Change management experience:
  - 5–14 yrs.—69 percent
  - 15+ yrs.—33 percent
- They change every twelve months or less.
- Change is triggered by three factors:
- They lose customers through:
  - Poor quality (92 percent);
  - Salespeople not following up (76.5 percent); and
  - Assuming they know what customers want (64.5 percent).

---

1 "Most Change Efforts Still Fail": the most recent source is *The Ken Blanchard Companies* in 2009.

What are the Meaningful Differences between Those Who Thrive on Change and Those Who Just Survive?

1.2. Why Write This Book Now?

Here's why we believe the time is right for this book.

- People are still the main reason for failed change by the executives surveyed. World economics are negatively impacting working and commercial relationships. Technology continues to deliver faster, opportunity-rich, and competitively challenging solutions that often impact jobs and working relationships. Change failure rates continue above 60 percent in North America and other global regions. So, working relationships are increasingly stressed as leaders drive to respond with speed and agility to competitive threats and opportunities.

The Cost of Failed Change

This book confirms that too many organizations today are still trying to do things differently, not *do different things*.

Failed change means lost opportunity, competitive vulnerability, poor revenues, lost employees, increased cynicism and fear. Its residue is a hostile and toxic culture, where change resistance becomes the norm.

So, why are these survey results important?

- Change management's track record isn't getting any better and, isn't likely to, if we don't do different things. Who says?

- Change failure rates continue above 60 percent

- Surveyed executives still say people are the main reason for failed change

- World economics are negatively impacting working and commercial relationships

- Technology continues to deliver faster, opportunity-rich and competitively challenging solutions that often impact jobs and working relationships.

A recent study discovered the following:

Costs of Failed Change
- **Fifty-six percent wrote off at least one IT project in twelve months.**
- **Average cost $12.5m USD**
- **Total $1.7 billion USD for this group alone**
- **Only 9 percent surveyed regard completing projects within budget as their most important success measurement!**

(KPMG study 2002 of 134 public companies)

Ninety-six percent of leaders say their current business models are misaligned with emergent realities, unforeseen challenges, and changing priorities. Two-thirds say "extensive changes" are required. Yet they also confess they don't know how to go about fixing what's no longer delivering sustainable competitive advantage.[2]

The cost of a failed change can be staggering, from lowering morale to losing key customers due to poor quality.[3]

We believe that it's time to challenge change management leaders to stand back. What follows is a summary of our conclusions, including questionnaires, organizational assessment, and action points drawn from the collective wisdom of over one thousand leaders, managers, and consultants with ten thousand collective years of change-management experience.

---

2 Chartered Accountants of Ontario—Refocusing the Organization, http://www.icao.on.ca
3 Ninety-six percent of our contributors; see A3.14: Most Common Reasons for Losing Customers.

Section 2: The Why and What of Change

2.1 Today's Context

Every one faces complexity driven by uncertainty and accelerating change. It is the "New Normal" making leadership more demanding and in demand.

Accelerating complexity places extreme demands on leaders. The leader's ability to relate, energize, and develop their followers is critical to empower them to act without direction. It's a competitive imperative and requires a new balance of more effective and affective leadership. It's the ability to produce results by being affective. That ability to influence people, in the way they think, feel and act is now paramount

> **"Leaders cannot afford to choose between reason and intuition, or head and heart, any more than they would choose to walk on one leg..."**
>
> (Peter Senge)

Surveys from IBM and KPMG give us some clues. Not surprisingly, CEOs are confronted with massive shifts caused by:

- New Government Regulations

- Increased information management.

- Changes in global economic power centers

- Accelerated industry transformation

- Rapidly evolving customer preferences

In the KPMG survey 1400 Corporate Decision Makers across 22 countries) showed:[4]

- 94 percent agreed that managing complexity is important to company success

- 70 percent agreed that increasing complexity is one of the biggest challenges their company faces

- Trying to manage complexity has had mixed success with only 40 percent of senior executives rating themselves as "very effective"

In IBM's annual survey, they interviewed 1,500 CEOs from 60 countries across 33 industries.[5]

Most say that successfully navigating increasing complexity requires creativity. Yet, less than half believed their enterprises are prepared to handle a highly volatile, increasingly complex business environment.

It doesn't sound as if things are getting any better. Since 1996, surveys have consistently shown that 60-70 percent change initiatives fail in North America fail and now more than 60 percent of CEOs said that industry transformation is the top factor contributing to uncertainty, indicating greater challenges to find more creative ways of managing organizations, finances, people and strategy.

In IBM's survey:

- 80 percent CEOs expect things to get much more complex but only 49 percent believe their organizations are equipped to deal with it successfully – the largest leadership challenge identified in eight years of research.

- Most say such constant change demands creativity

They say they need creative leaders that will:

- Focus much more on innovation

---

4 KPMG Confronting Complexity May 2011
5 IBM Capitalizing on Complexity Global CEO Study 2010

- Be more comfortable with ambiguity and experiment with new business models to realize their strategies

- Invite disruptive innovation and take balanced risk

- Consider changing their enterprise drastically to enable innovation

- Engage their teams to be courageous enough to alter their status quo

- What have the "stand out" organizations been doing as this trend has emerged?

Standout Organizations

Over last 5 years, IBM showed that "stand-out" organizations buck this trend

- 54 percent are more likely than others to make rapid decisions.

- 95 percent identified getting closer to customers as a strategic imperative

- 20 percent more of their future revenue will be from new sources than their more traditional peers due to their superior operating dexterity

- 61 percent see "global thinking" is a top leadership quality.

- Most see the need for new industry models and skills as they can't rely on models they use in their domestic markets

In parallel, 74 percent KMPG respondents see opportunity in complexity, like:

- Gaining competitive advantage,

- Creating better strategies,

- Developing new markets,

- Driving efficiency,

- Bringing in new products.

They also see complexity driving new approaches to HR, geographic expansion, mergers/acquisitions and outsourcing. Typical reactions to increasing these complexities are curious.

As these surveys show, many leaders see their world as complex but the questions is: Do their organizations need to be complex as result? The increased pressure we find has an insidious effect of CEOs feeling that they need more control, more systems, more technology, more….complexity and often fall prey to:

> **"The perfect becoming the enemy of the good"**
>
> (Voltaire)

Let's unpack this. As technology gets faster and cheaper, pressured decision makers seek more data and information which locks them away from the future. The real danger is developing corporate myopia that focuses on refining existing products while competitors are developing "Game Changers"

Added to this is a common view that more data and information gathering capabilities reduces uncertainty. But, time-compressed decision-making rests on identifying your competitors' intentions with the least amount of information to take action first. The need is for enough situational awareness to find competitive vulnerabilities and predict their actions.

The problem is that the time to create the future is compressed. Only wisdom deals with the future. But achieving wisdom isn't easy. For people to acquire wisdom they must transition through data, then information, then knowledge to get to wisdom – "evaluated understanding" Let me explain

Wisdom is understanding where none has existed before. Unlike data, information and knowledge, it asks questions which have no known answer. Wisdom is a human state informed by technology, not replaced by it, and enabled by future perfect and future worse-case thinking. The challenge is leading people through transitions of understanding data, to information, to knowledge, and finally to wisdom – fast enough to be useful.

> "The only sustainable competitive advantage is
> an organization's ability to learn faster than the competition."
>
> Peter Senge

This means that leaders need to create learning organizations that acquire wisdom fast enough to thrive in rapid change by:

1. Creating cultures that support ongoing employee learning, critical thinking, and risk taking with new ideas

2. Allowing mistakes and valuing employee contributions

3. Learning by experience and experiment

4. Dispersing newly gained wisdom through the organization and embedding it into the day-to-day

In later sections, you will see that these survey's clarion call for changing how organizations should be led falls on many leaders' deaf ears. With this context in mind, we now look at our survey's findings of how often both initiated and reactive change occurs. These findings are an important confirmation of both the KMPG and IBM findings on the increasing rapidity and complexity of change. It is important because it increases the risks of each failed change impacting each subsequent change in a compressed timeframe.

This section summarizes 781 contributors' two thousand replies to three questions:

*   How often does your organization initiate change?

*   Why do we need to change?

*   What does change mean to you?

2.2 How often does your organization initiate change?

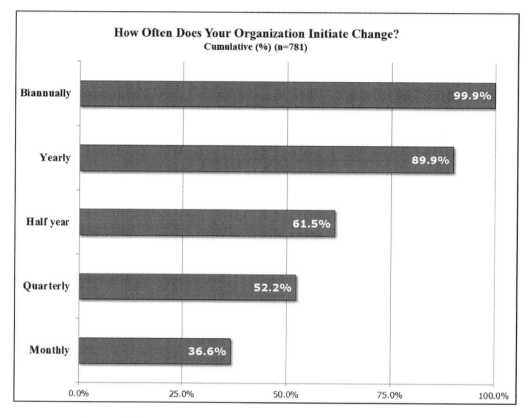

CHART 1: HOW OFTEN DOES YOUR ORGANIZATION INITIATE CHANGE?

It's interesting to note that contributors also made 248 additional comments. The reader will notice that we asked how often does your organization "initiate change"

For many contributors, they clearly live in a more reactive world. Here's a summary of their comments.

- As needed, by customers, projects, markets, governments, poor performance, environmental factors (83)

- Constant, Ongoing, Process (63)

- Hard to Say, Infrequently, Not predictable (20)

- Reactive (5)

Add to these figures those who say their organizations change at least monthly (36.6 percent)

Here are some contributor comments of change's continuous nature:

- Reviews of strategy expectations with actual market achievement

- Sporadic, but too often.

- There is no specific agenda. It happens as and when a need is felt. Firefight like situation.

- Too much. It is not effective because it is the company driven, not employee driven.

- We are constantly innovating and continually improving programs, processes, resources and our approach

- We are growing rapidly and are always evolving our services so that they better serve the needs of our clients.

- We are in a continuous mode. We strive for the most current best practices and encourage innovation in the 11 different regions we work across.

- We are in constant motion; it's is part of our culture

- We are looking all the time to see how we can grow

- We sometimes daily to adapt to new situations - a benefit of being a small company

2.3 Why do we need to change?

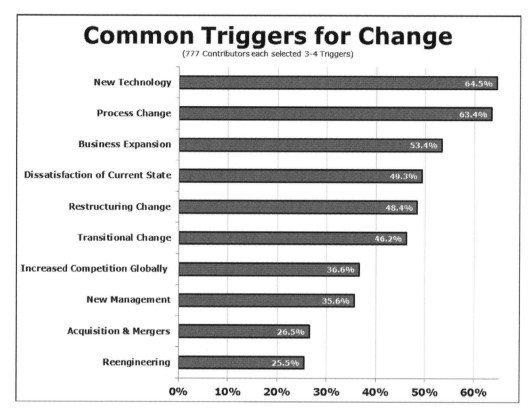

Common Triggers for Change
(777 Contributors each selected 3-4 Triggers)

Trigger	Percentage
New Technology	64.5%
Process Change	63.4%
Business Expansion	53.4%
Dissatisfaction of Current State	49.3%
Restructuring Change	48.4%
Transitional Change	46.2%
Increased Competition Globally	36.6%
New Management	35.6%
Acquisition & Mergers	26.5%
Reengineering	25.5%

CHART 2: COMMON TRIGGERS FOR CHANGE

Despite some contributors finding these questions obvious, many others didn't find them obvious at all. Results elsewhere in this report support this opinion and show there are often gaps between change planning and implementation, resulting from not addressing these questions. For many contributors this gap fuels people's natural

> **Frankly, no company can fix everything, leverage all opportunities, and satisfy all complaints. In business it will always be about making choices—some from experience, some from market pressures, and some from best guesses. We hope that all choices are made with the intent to improve results, but few choices will be without friction.**
>
> (Contributor comment)

resistance, such as when they get conflicting messages. This condition is growing in importance as the ever-increasing rate of change demands that leaders give clear and compelling reasons for employees to overcome their feelings, such as the following:

"Here we go again," as one contributor commented.

Like this contributor, others understand the crucial nature of credibility based on the clarity of what leaders say and how they address the first question on people's minds:

Is this change really necessary?

Answers to this question run from organizational, operational, market to competitive reasons. Apart some contributor's exhortations to *change or die,* here are other commentaries we hope are more useful.

2.4. The Change Context

This context for effectively communicating the *what and why of change* relies on awareness of the time needed and the difficulty of three types of change:

- Internal processes,

- Internal culture and

- External pressures, like changes in legislation.[6]

Of course, all three can come into play at the same time, and businesses not responding simultaneously will make their survival a struggle.

The challenge for the keepers of the *What* of change is communicating in ways that result in the following:

- Reduce operational complacency;

- Improve competitiveness;

---

6   Here and elsewhere throughout *Focusing Change to Win*, contributors' responses to our survey may be lightly edited for clarity.

- Enable constructive criticism;

- Build trust;

- Improve their relationships;

- Help deliver products that competitively meet customers' needs.

2.5. The What of Change—
Ten Best Practices to Communicate Change

(Summary of 2000 comments on how to communicate change)

THE WHAT AND WHY OF CHANGE:
TEN BEST PRACTICES TO COMMUNICATE CHANGE

1. Identify the change benefits before implementation. Use them as motivators linked to individual and team achievement recognition.

2. Demonstrate to stakeholders and employees that the organization can respond faster to customer demands.

3. Explain how human and financial resources will be aligned within the organization.

4. Show people how change impacts will be assessed and demonstrate how future change readiness will manage them.

5. Explain how improved organizational effectiveness and efficiency can be maintained and improved by acknowledging employee concerns.

6. Demonstrate your confidence in knowledgeable employees and improved relations with trade unions and regulators.

7. Explain how to reduce implementation risks.

8. Detail how the plan will develop best practices, leaders, and teams.

9. Outline how communication and management information will be improved and what role this information will play in improving efficiency (e.g., less waste, fewer blockages and duplication).

10. Detail the awards and recognition for people who show commitment to the change.

2.6. The Why of Change

Why Change—A Contributor's View
One contributor quoted Chase LeBlanc's blog If You Can't Stand Friction, Get Outta the Kitchen, which captures many contributors' feelings about change. Here are some excerpts:

- Ilya Prigogine (who received the Nobel Prize in chemistry) contends that friction is a fundamental property of nature, and nothing grows without it: not mountains, pearls, or people. He suggested that it is the capacity to withstand being shaken that is the key to growth. Any structure at the molecular, organizational, or psychological level that is isolated from disturbance (and therefore change) is also protected from friction and thus from growth.

- This serves as a reminder. Change is not the enemy—inactivity, incapability, and inflexibility are. Any change will generate friction. This friction will serve you best if you use it to grow wiser and better, more competent and responsible.

- Friction and then growth is the natural order. Workplace change is inevitable; constantly evolving business conditions are realities for everyone.

For many, the starting point is the one-minute elevator pitch that asks why change or, more to the point, What if we don't change?

**What are the implications of not changing? -
Sample explanations for employees**
Here are some contributor examples to consider when communicating with employees:

- Without change our organization becomes stagnant. We are unable to adjust to the environment around us in order to keep pace with our potential customers' needs.

- Our past passions become dim and we may lose sight of what we are really striving for. Change allows us to widen our horizon and deepen our understanding.

- We would not be able to adapt to an ever changing marketplace and we would lose our competitive advantage.

- If nothing moves forward, we cannot get better neither do we become a market leader.

- We will stagnate and competition will get ahead.

- Change is not a choice; it is like living with time. So, if we don't change, we will go out of business.

- We will be left behind competitively because change is a constant that affects everything and everyone.

- If we stay the same, we are losing ground. The world is fast moving and to keep pace, we must always be willing and aware of what changes must be implemented.

- If we keep doing what we've always done, we won't get the same results, we'll get further behind.

- If we stay still and static we will fall behind, change is not needed for changes sake but even the smallest change can make a big difference.

- As one contributor put it:

- Business is a race, and you need to change constantly in order to lead. Any change a process is cognitive, perpetual and generates learning. It's critical to our health and viability.

2.7 What Do We Need to Change?

We need change in an effort to explore new market positions, find new ways, to stop boredom, to improve, to be creative and to dream. Sometimes change is forced on us because funding, legislation and Government change.

2.7.1 Need to Change
- It's what makes us human. It is the only real constant that makes us alive in this world.

- We must be able to adapt and leverage change that is thrust upon us to improve.

2.7.2 Need to Adapt:
- We must adapt to new market conditions and improve conditions within the company; to technology and best practices; to different market conditions, economics, and demographics. We must stay current and adapt to changing circumstances in our environment or be replaced by a competitor or new agent. We need to adapt to market dynamics, customer requirements, and increasing demand. We must adapt to changing times, so that our customer gets the best value from every single penny they spend for the future. Our feelings and emotions are changing day by day, and adaptation is the most importing thing.

2.7.3 Company Survival:
- Remaining relevant and appropriate for the environment; ensuring our competitiveness, growth, innovativeness continues to support our longevity.

- Ensuring we continue to meet the new client demands and to seek improvement otherwise we risk stagnating and dying.

2.8.4 Improvement:
- Keep up with evolving trends. Satisfy customers consistently. Build a competitively winning business. Reduce costs. Satisfy more employees. Build profits by providing better service. Develop people's performance. Operate more effectively. Raise quality standards. Innovate throughout the value chain. Keep motivating. Develop more cohesive teams and align all people with your goals.

2.8 Summary

Contributors readily see the need for change to adapt, survive or improve. The world's ever-increasing pace demands that leaders give clear and compelling reasons for employees to overcome their feelings of *here we go again*. That response begs the question: What can leaders do about this condition. What follows are some thoughts.

All those implementing change know in advance, to some extent, that a change will be stressful and that not everyone will be willing to engage. For example, people often work well under certain stress to increase productivity. But, under other circumstances, they are surprised at the stress that another aspect of change can induce. So, stress can be negative, positive or neutral. For example, passing in an examination can be just stressful as failing. The problem occurs when people are under excessive or prolonged stress – *Unhealthy Stress*. The challenge for change leaders is that stress is unique and personal. A situation may be stressful for someone, but the same situation may be challenging for others.

If you look at the above comments, what sense of connection do you have between what people are expecting others to,

- *Stop doing*

- *Start doing*

- *Continue doing*

Notice that people rarely mention all three in the same contribution. Why is this important? All three expectations together create increased stress and potentially change resistance. It works like this.

> **Unhealthy Stress**
> **This occurs when people *think* that a change will demand personal commitments in excess of their mental and physical resources.**

Assuming we are always managing change with limited resources such as people, money, technology, and time, leaders have to manage the tension between these three elements of ***stop, start,*** and ***continue***. After analyzing contributor comments, there are clearly those who understand this condition and those who do not. The critical point is that, after deciding the commercial and organizational need for change, leaders need the emotional intelligence[7] to identify which groups and individuals are likely to experience unhealthy stress and resistance.

The leaders' role in producing sustainable change requires them to understand and be capable of managing these stresses *consistently*. It makes sense to keep people focused on the three change behaviors: namely, what you want people to stop, start, and

---

7   John D. Mayer and Peter Salovey. Emotional Intelligence (EI) is "the ability to monitor one's own and others' feelings and emotions, to discriminate among them and to use this information to guide one's thinking and actions." Research on EI suggests that good emotional understanding, especially in leaders, leads to increased social effectiveness and therefore increases the chance of change success.

continue doing. This sets a framework that grounds worker stress into a more objective and manageable framework.

Many contributors comment on leaders' inconsistency and how it fuels people's natural resistance to change, whereas constant communication focused on individuals about the *why and what of change* is fundamental to sustainable change.

We conclude that people's change resistance is often the result of stress. Such stress is reduced when people understand what is expected of them and what is not. Similarly, leaders get stressed for the same reasons during a change. Stressed leaders often treat and react to their people with spiraling consequences. So leaders need to establish what people expect of them and what they don't.

The process chart opposite shows how we see handling stress and resistance.

2.6. Action Points 1: Reducing Employee Stress to Manage Change Resistance

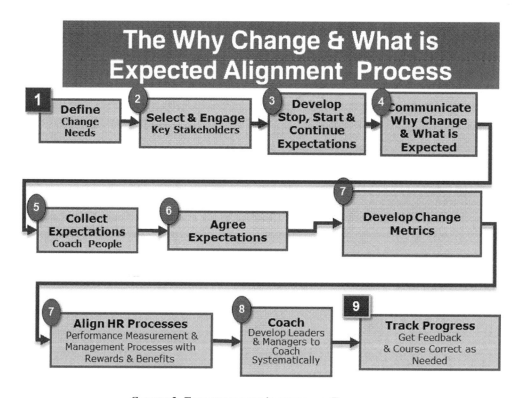

CHART 3: EXPECTATION ALIGNMENT PROCESS

Here are some action points to start using the *change expectations framework* with your change leaders.

Action Points 1: Reducing Employee Stress to Manage Change Resistance

Most contributor responses indicate that their organizations change anywhere from daily to annually. These changes are often unique to the organization, the triggers for change, and how change is managed. Yet all change has three things in common.

The Three Common Elements of All Change

Defining your own change and how it is managed starts with the following:
- Identifying what you expect people to stop doing, so that they can start doing new things
- Specifying what you expect people to start doing
- Confirming what you want people to continue doing, while continuing to coordinate and keep the organization running.

Focus on communicating constantly the *why of change and what is expected* for your change to be effective *and* communicate what the change is *not* about. This is the change expectations framework, which engages deeper understanding and helps everyone manage stress more effectively.

Just in case you think everyone does these three steps, you are probably wrong at least 70 percent of the time, according to studies over the last ten years.

ACTION POINTS 1: REDUCING EMPLOYEE STRESS TO MANAGE CHANGE RESISTANCE

Section 3: Why Do People Resist Change?

3.1. Introduction

Since change management became popular, failures have left their mark on our contributors over the last eight years. It seems, through their eyes, resistance is a brown field site.[8] Gone is the naïveté of *a job for life* and the enduring contract between leaders and other stakeholders. Now change is synonymous with downsizing, doing more for less, and so on.

The accelerated organizational change demands more of everyone. Such reorganizations have major consequences for employees. Accelerated change failure creates cultural toxicity. That's why many experience FUD (fear, uncertainty, and doubt) when they detect another change is on the way. This causes leaders to identify this condition as change resistance.

> ### Change Resistance Definition
> *Change resistance* **is the actions people take when they think that a change threatens them. The key words here are "think" and "threatens."**
>
> **The threat need not be real or large for resistance to occur. Resistance can take many forms, including active or passive, overt or covert, individual or organized, and aggressive or passive.**
>
> **It comes down to peoples' sense of security and the extent to which they feel secure as an employee. The more people feel insecure, the more resistant they will become.**

Here's the reality: leaders need employee support and trust if company change is going to stand any chance of success. Our results underscore this. If people are cynical about a change, pessimism will set in, and failure is assured.

---

8   Brown field sites are industrial and commercial facilities available for reuse where redevelopment of such a facility may be complicated by real or perceived environmental contaminations. The land may be contaminated by low concentrations of hazardous waste or pollution but has the potential to be reused once it is cleaned up. (adapted from Wikipedia)

Our findings underscore the multifaceted nature of planning and implementing change. There are no simple remedies, sound bites, or grizzly seven-step plan. Yet at its core, effective change management has fundamental values that, if believed in, will provide a sound basis for planning and executing change.

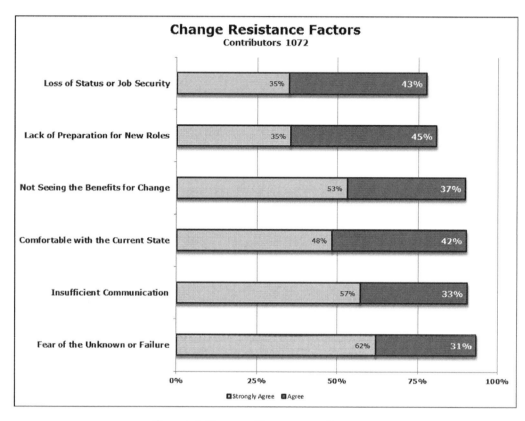

CHART 4: CHANGE RESISTANCE FACTORS

3.2. Why Do People Resist Change?

Contributors to the chart above paint a vivid picture of change resistance. FUD (93 percent) and insufficient communication (90 percent) lend further evidence to the legacy of failed change, economic turbulence, and rapid technological change. This level of stress, when combined with people being *comfortable with their current state* (90 percent) and *not seeing the benefits for change* (90 percent), presents a significant obstacle for these change leaders. Such consistently high ratings across eighty countries sends a clear warning which a communication agenda very clearly for those who really want to improve their chances of successful change.

These contributors paint a picture of failed change, broken trust, fractured communication, and poor leadership. We summarize their comments as follows:

- Failed change and cultural toxicity: If people don't trust you, what chance do you stand?

- People can't be bothered: "What's in it for me?"

- Not knowing the purpose of it all, poor leadership embeds and accelerates resistance.

3.2.1. Failed Change and Cultural Toxicity

Here are some contributors' comments on the impact of too many failed attempts:

- Sometimes change fatigue occurs due to too much change and unsuccessful change.

- Employees are cynical due to previous changes being mismanaged or oversold.

- Employees feel there are always threats, never see a window of opportunity, see negative consequences of change and are not being disabused by management.

- In the United States, more often than not, change equals layoffs. For the employees that remain, it's more work for the same pay.

- Employees' resistance to change is different for each employee; it can be influenced with leadership communication, but ultimately it's the employees' call as to whether change: they can accept or refuse. Allowing people to come and go and find their rightful place should be the attitude of management. People who do match change will come, while people who don't will go.

- Cultural toxicity can be aggravated when technology and change reduces the employees required without increasing company profitability.

- Working as a team is crucial to overcoming resistance.

3.2.2. If People Don't Trust You, What Chance Do You Stand?

While contributors didn't make this link, it seems a reasonable conclusion to draw that failed change breeds mistrust. Mistrust permeates leadership and compromises promised outcomes and a change's value.

Here's a contributor sampling:

> **Why can't people be bothered?**
>
> Gone is the naïveté of *a job for life* and the enduring contract between leaders and other stakeholders. Now change is synonymous with downsizing, doing more for less, and so on.

- There is a lack of management sincerity when they try to sell change as good for people who (in fact) will be losing security and certainty.

- People love change. What they hate is manipulation, coercion, arbitrary force, or social engineering.

- Employees have a fear of letting the old ways go and trusting something new.

FUD (Fear, Uncertainty, and Doubt)

For some, resistance comes from fear, uncertainty, and doubt. For these people change means an unsettled state when, for example,

- They feel little control;

- They fear losing their jobs; and

- They feel they will have a reduced status.

Lack of Respect

Management's not respecting employees also creates mistrust:

- Management has a tendency to assume employees lack intelligence.

- Leaders don't trust employees and their loyalty to the organization; leaders need to respect people more and help them find their way.

Role Clarity

- Employees are not sure of their role/responsibility in a new organizational structure and don't understand their new roles or responsibilities. There are no apparent rewards or consequences for changing. Employees worry how the change will affect their personal work. If employees understand the need for change and how it will affect them, they will be more willing to adapt.

3.2.3. People Can't Be Bothered

In contrast, some contributors felt that change resistance lay in the people rather than in the change process itself. It's a bit like the chicken and the egg—*we don't know who came first*, but here are some comments to get another perspective on change resistance:

- People do not like change. Positive attitudes to change are missing, and the reason why is because people can't be bothered. Much of my corporate life was in a company where many did this, and it showed.

- Many people are lazy and change implies extra effort.

- Employees working for a company for a long time are stuck and too lazy to move.

- Some people fight change by their nature, while others embrace change—it's how we are wired.

- One person concludes that there are change lovers—those who will change under pressure—and those who will never change, not even under immense threat and pressure.

- It means some people must be let go immediately, as change follows change.

- People lack common sense, digging in their heels and not wanting to see reality or truth.

- There's no "will to perform," a lack of which also results in resistance. This does, however, contradict the point of

3.2.4. What's in It for Me?

Needless to say, change resistance increases when people can't answer the above question. Here are some contributor comments:

- [Employees] can't see real-world applications for their day-to-day lives—is it because they are not looking? The case [for change] is often not made in terms of the individual.

- Not knowing what's in it for me (WIIFM).

- The benefits they will receive from the change do not match the effort that will be required. Risk assessments, in the minds of most, don't link to potential opportunities.

3.2.5. Not Knowing the Purpose

Here those responding highlight the gap between what's in leaders' minds and their employees. Contributors here draw distinctions between insufficient, inconsistent, and inappropriate communication.

- There is inappropriate communication, such as too much emphasis on what goes badly and needs improvement.

- There is not enough support or understanding of how exactly to function well in the changed environment or job.

- Top management considers changes to be proprietary; yet without collaboration, chances for communication failure increase.

- Employees don't understand what the change means in specific terms, so one can adapt.

The employees will not fear change when they understand that they are an important part of making change successful.

As one person put it,

- "If you don't understand the staff's communication styles, you will be in a worse position. We all need things explained in different ways—some need facts, some need details, some need support and consultation, and others need ideas and possibilities."

And finally, when contributors comment on poor communication, they always come back to the following problems:

- People's lack of involvement in both planning and implementation

- Leaders' inability to develop a shared understanding of their change strategy

3.3. Lack of Involvement

Many contributors imply that *no one is naturally resistant to change* and, for some, change resistance means that leaders have not found *effective ways of partnering with people in the change journey*. Not being involved, for many, reinforces a negative view of leader's inability or unwillingness to involve others: For example, not being part of the decision process and not being given a *stake in it* results in comments such as the following:

- Being "done to"

- "I do not feel that I matter" and a feeling of "taking it [change] personally"

- Other comments are more specific about when they want involvement:

- Not being involved in change preparation in initiating and planning; not getting those affected involved in the problem solving quickly enough

3.4. Poor Leadership Embeds and Accelerates Change Resistance

The most commented area was on how poor leadership embeds and accelerates change resistance. Contributor comments indicate the following:

- Poor change management; lacking leadership basic skills; leaders' attitudes toward their work and those they lead

3.5. Poor Change Management

Several contributors criticized their leader's structure, planning, and execution of change processes:

- People are down on what they are not clearly caught up on.

- [Resistance] stems from a weak value system; there's a lack of coherence in various change initiatives that also lack coordination; there's a lack of follow-through with the previous change before they switch gears again.

- There is poor preparation of both stakeholders and poor development of change sponsors; there's no support for the new management and not enough support and understanding of how exactly to function well in the changed environment or job.

- There is no anticipating the time needed to get people on board and no setting up and properly "selling" requirements and expectations. There is, however, imposed change that happens without transition.

- There is no capacity to deal with the change and training required.

3.6. Lack of Leadership Skills

Some contributors seemed to differentiate the change process from the leader's behavior during the change process. Here are some typical examples:

- Buy-in at the top not clear.

- If employees get consistent messages from all levels, they will move with the change.

- It takes only one manager to be not on board, and the whole process can be unraveled. Resistance to change occurs at top level of management (owners) first; if change can be avoided, they will push all the way.

- Our leadership culture is always following the latest flavor of the day (manufactured) change ideas.

Others comment on the lack of basic leadership skills: Too much emphasis on what goes badly and needs improvement. Management has a tendency to assume its employees lack intelligence. There is a lack of leadership skills to take employees on the journey. Stale managers who fear change and who want to control their empire. Employee leaders don't walk the talk. There is weak and ineffective leadership from ineffectual leaders.

3.7 Rebuilding Trust is the Cornerstone for Change Readiness

Globally there is a slow erosion of those binding forces for people to "go that extra mile". The employee-employer psychological contract is degrading. The degree to which people identify with their job and consider job performance as important to their self-worth is slipping. In our survey; contributors identified the main culprits as:

- Poor Planning

- Lack of Leadership

- Inconsistent leadership

- Poor Implementation

- Lack of Adaptability

- Lack of Communication

- Lack of Control

More than ever, we need to repair, build and protect the trust people have in their employers.

In North America, our evidence from 8 expectation alignment projects ranging from Royal Bank of Canada through Nature Conservancy to Turner Construction shows a clear trend. Leaders consistently under-estimate the gap between what they expect of their managers and what people think is expected of them. In all studies, leaders had 65 percent+ more expectations than their people were aware.

In the UK, managers need to do more if they want to earn employee trust, according to the latest survey into employee attitudes from the Chartered Institute of Personnel and Development (CIPD). Trust in senior management is declining, particularly in the private sector, with

- Only 25 percent employees willing to place a lot of trust in senior management to look after their interests and

- Only 41 percent placing little or no trust in them to do so.

Essentially, new research suggests that many employees are losing faith in their management yet it seems leaders don't connect this condition with losing ground competitively.

According to the Employee Outlook 2012 survey from the Chartered Institute for Personnel and Development (CIPD), corporate scandals are "eroding trust" in leaders with possible damaging impacts on staff engagement and the job market.

Any wonder then, why the report revealed that 58 percent of employees display signs of being "not bothered" about quality.

Unsurprisingly, those who display "neutral engagement" are:

- Only half as likely to "go the extra mile" than those who are fully engaged in their roles, and

- Three times more likely to be looking for a new job

- Less knowledgeable about their organization's core purpose

Peter Cheese, Chief Executive at the CIPD, said it was perhaps unsurprising to see trust in the workplace eroding, given the number of examples of "unethical behaviour and corrosive cultures" overseen by senior leaders in the recent months. As the survey shows:

- Only 36 percent of respondents said that they trusted the senior leaders in their organisation

- Only 40 percent were satisfied that they had the chance to express their ideas and views to those higher up.

> "What's worrying is the impact this will have on engagement. We know that strong employee engagement drives higher productivity and better business outcomes, so such a prominent display of 'neutral engagement' in the workplace should act as a real wake up call for employers".
>
> "Now more than ever, organisations need to pay close attention to the impact the behaviours of senior leaders is having on the rest of the workforce and consider how they can improve corporate culture from the top down," he concluded."
>
> (Peter Cheese, CIPD)

A recent study from the UK Government's Department for Business, Innovation and Skills stated that a lack of strong leadership and management is stunting the growth if the UK job market.

These threats to productivity and competitiveness depend on leaders focusing on aligning their expectations for change and what their people think is expected.

> "It takes more than personal integrity to build trust.... It takes skills, smart supporting processes, and unwavering top manager focus."
>
> (HBR, 2003, Feb – by Robert Galford & Anne Seibold Drapeau)

Alignment needs to focus on the building blocks of trust. They are not new, yet leaders often do not pay close enough attention to:

- Consistency – "Walking their own talk"

- Clear Communication – Translating what changes really mean"

- Showing a willingness to work through disagreements

3.7.1 The Enemy at the Gate – The Need for Alignment

Many times a lack of trust is not immediately obvious. But, you know when the "Enemy is at the Gate". When you hear people say:

- "Why haven't you done it?"

- "I thought you were doing that"

- "They never tell us in-time!'

- "Why are you doing that – it's my job!"

They often stem from:

- Inconsistent Messages (with leader's behaviour especially)

- Inconsistent Standards – people perceive favoritism

- Misplaced Kindness – Managers not confronting incompetence and negativity.

- False Feedback – saying someone is doing great when they are not.

- Elephants in the parlor – the issue that no-one wants to acknowledge or talk about them.

- Rumors in a vacuum – unfounded yet damaging

Mike Emmett, CIPD Employee Relations Adviser in UK says,

> **"Trust is a key element in the psychological contract between employers and employees. If employees have a positive psychological contract, this means they will show higher levels of satisfaction, motivation and commitment to the organization."**

Our research endorses others work in showing these factors are important in helping employers reduce absence, retain staff and solve recruitment difficulties. So if employees don't trust their employer, or don't feel fairly treated, they will display a lack of commitment and underperformance.

A recent survey shows that employers need to work a lot harder to get the best from their staff. Good communication is key- consulting people about change and ensuring they feel involved in the decision making - is basic good management. But too many firms are not getting the basics right. People are not clear or confident in what their leaders expect of them, especially in times of change

It is not only top management who have problems - trust in employees' immediate line manager has also declined, dropping in the private sector by over 10 percent over the past two years. Furthermore, fewer than half of respondents say their supervisor motivates them and only 37 percent say their line manager actually helps them improve performance.

3.7.2 The Ultimate Enemy - Stress

Misaligned expectations are often stressors in the psychological contract. Stress can have huge costs for employers in terms of sickness absence, productivity and morale.

A recent report explored the characteristics of a high quality workplace. This has to do with the demands of the job, personal control, and support from supervisors or colleagues, work relationships, clarity of role and degree of change in the workplace. The success of these six dimensions significantly impacts motivation, organizational commitment, and satisfaction at work and customer loyalty. People who scored highly on these characteristics reported much lower levels of work-related stress.

These findings suggest that managers need to make significant further efforts to tackle the issues responsible for creating stress: basically issues about good management.

> "The survey findings suggest that UK Companies is failing to put in place management practices that address the root causes of work-related stress. This is not a "feel-good" issue about being nice to employees. It is an issue about productivity and getting the best out of the workforce. The survey underlines once again that dealing with stress is an issue about performance and profitability."
>
> "These findings suggest that managers have a significant job on their hands in motivating a majority of their workforce."
>
> (Mike Emmett)

The need for leaders to ensure their people understand, agree and are committed to what they expect is obvious yet often overlooked. What is not so obvious is the leader's need to elicit and respond to what employees expect of them. This should be a process, not a survey.

It is far more active and genuinely engaging than surveys or other passive methods. It needs to compare each employee's expectations and their assumptions with others in the organization, in regard to a specific change.

Such explicit and specific alignment of expectations and assumptions is the fundamental to building the transparency and consistency essential for a trusting environment. And a trusting environment is the very basis for productivity and competitiveness.

3.8. Action Points 2: Managing Change Stress and Resistance

All these contributors are saying that change resistance is natural, but you don't need to make it that difficult if you do some things profoundly well.

This starts with recognizing that change resistance is caused by stress. So why not treat the cause and not the symptom? Stress is natural and good if managed. Stress is reduced if leaders create clear and consistent frameworks that help people make informed decisions about committing to a change or not. Here's how we interpret what our contributors are saying:

Action Points 2: Managing Change Resistance Protocols & Values

Protocols
- Clarifying the Direction:
- Leaders clarify their change's what, why, how, and WIIFMs[1] for different groups and individuals. Once understood, leaders then move into a process of addressing peoples' questions, such as *What does this mean for me?* This leads to aligning expectations.
- Aligning Expectations:
- This is a process flow in two directions between leaders and each individual. It starts with leader's specifying for each person those activities and behaviors that they expect him or her to stop, start, or continue doing. Then leaders encourage the reciprocal: people specifying expectations of their leaders. Then leaders cement these agreements with mutual accountabilities.
- Developing Accountabilities:
- This step develops the rewards and consequences through performance measurement, management, and rewards that ensure expectations of *both* leaders and their people are met.

Values

These are sound practices for reducing and managing peoples' stress and resistance, but only if leaders have realized the importance of *walking their own talk* and demonstrated the following:
- Consistency: Being consistent and transparent is crucial to let those who remain see leaders act accordingly.
- Respect: Leaders show respect for their people, and people for their leaders.
- Communication: Using every means and media to help engage people, not just tell them where to be on Monday at 8:00 a.m.
- Honesty: The corporate good is not served by those who don't want to give change their best try, at least for a period. Leaders need to be open and candid.

[1] WIIFM = What's In It For Me

ACTION POINTS 2: MANAGING CHANGE STRESS AND RESISTANCE

Section 4: Why Bother Measuring Change?

To many the answer to the above question may seem obvious. But, before you turn the page, read the contributors' comments that follow:

- Why measure change, anyway?

- What are the problems of measuring change?

- What measures should we select?

- Was measuring change worth it? Did we get the ROI we were looking for?

- What can we learn from using change metrics?

- What works to measure change, and what doesn't?

- What does it take to navigate change?

- How can measuring change help align our people?

- What do metrics do for improving what we do?

- How do metrics help us sell change?

- How do metrics help keep our customers?

- How do metrics help gain and retain market share?

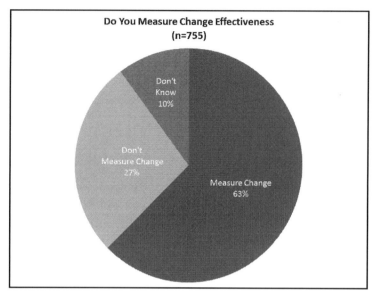

CHART 5: DO YOU MEASURE CHANGE EFFECTIVENESS?

Most of our contributors do measure change, yet 37 percent either don't measure change, or they don't know. So, here's some evidence that this issue is not the no-brainer many think it to be.

CHART 6: HOW WELL DO YOU MEASURE CHANGE MANAGEMENT PROCESSES?

From this chart, those that do measure the four areas specified say they are very effective or effective in measuring customer satisfaction, efficiency, productivity, and profitability. Yet only 57 percent say this of capturing markets.

This response begs the question of why they are more effective at measuring customer satisfaction than theoretically easier areas of measurement such as profitability.

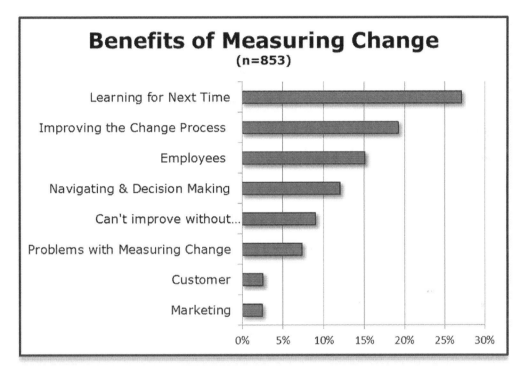

CHART 7: BENEFITS OF MEASURING CHANGE

In the chart above, we can see what our contributor's value in measuring the change process and its outcomes. It is interesting to note again that learning is so highly rated in contrast to an apparent lack of focus on learning vehicles such as coaching, mentoring, and training. It's also worth pointing out that those contributors who report "Problems with Measuring Change" (7.3 percent) feel that measuring change is too difficult or not worth it. The other striking disconnect is the low number of people who see benefits to both marketing and customers. This is curious, as the most common reason contributors give for losing customers does not relate to price but to quality (92.2 percent), poor follow-up by salespeople (76.5 percent) and making the wrong assumptions about customers (64.5 percent). It would seem that the relationship between change and competitive advantage is not as clearly connected as one might think.

4.1. Why Measure Change, Anyway?

Here's a distillation of contributors' comments on what happens if you don't measure change:

- Nothing gets done—that is where it ends.

- You will never know if the change worked or got results you like or intended.

- You can't manage what you don't measure.

- You have no idea of a change's success or failure.

- You can't determine effectiveness.

- You will stop making progress.

- You won't know if the change was needed at all.

- You will waste time and scrap the change too late.

- Management will continue to believe it was a success and then damage morale.

Overall, many contributors are clear on the consequences of not measuring change progress and results. They stress the need to observe and manage their effectiveness. Such results can then be shared with employees, so they can learn and use for future change initiatives.

Making performance visible is valuable for increasing change success, be it productivity, profitability, performance, or morale.

An integral part of sustained success is using specific and measurable outcomes to increase a change's credibility and for future initiatives. Being able to show short-term wins early and end results lets executives and others know if you are heading in the right direction, if not what adjustments are needed.

Metrics help assess change success, so you can adjust change parameters as needed. This is important, as there is far less value in knowing after the fact the extent of success or failure. For most people metrics are most valuable if they prompt early course corrections. They should not only provide means to compare goals to actual results but also compare and contrast other means to achieve goals. This leads some to advocate establishing benchmarks.

4.1.2. Benchmarking

Metrics themselves are most useful if a baseline is established to allow before- and after-results comparisons. This enables more timely and effective management if you are using the right tools and KPIs (key performance indicators). Crucially, many look to seeing their change develop and making timely adjustments when expected results are not being met. They see that benchmarks are useful for the following:

- Showing your change process is successful

- Informing your employee, suppliers, and customers

- Celebrating results with your employees and praising their efforts

- Justifying future similar investments, especially if the program was complex

- Calibrating the degree of success or failure

- Making the change tangible and real

- Providing visibility and credibility for the change

As many point out, metrics and benchmarks are only useful if they satisfy the following criteria:

- Are robustly measured—guesswork won't prove a business case, much less justify a project's success

- Allow the organization to correct course to ensure that the change meets the desired objectives

- Help understand what the barriers and resistors are with respect to the change

Again, as you read these obvious points, we ask that you dwell a moment on what they are saying. In summary, contributors stress that before embarking on change, you need the following:

- Clear objectives

- Specific desired benefits

- Agreed-upon quality levels you expect to achieve

Only then, should you decide what to continuously measure, monitor, and manage to ensure your company is more effective. Each metric should do the following:

- Get timely and accurate feedback

- Gauge progress to understand where you are in the process

- Allow managing each objective

- Tell you when each objective is reached

- Tell you when the change is fully implemented

- Identify what's working and what isn't (on a scale that is relevant)

- Identify how well your process is working

- Quantify if you're really saving money, time, improving customer satisfaction, and so on

- Measure only things that can be improved

4.2. What Are the Problems of Measuring Change?

For some the idea of specifying what metrics to use is situational. Others are skeptical of the current metrics used.

4.2.1. Problems with Measuring Change Benefits

Others criticize the poor linkages between their performance indicators and measuring the impact of change management:

- It's focused on analysis of a specific intervention rather than a system-based approach—still; it helps validate the continuation of change management processes.

- Given great levels of volatility, uncertainty, and risks, if metrics aren't comprehensive and ongoing, you lose sight of your mission, vision, profitability, and sustainability.

- Accurately gauging progress and results depends on isolating them from changes in other variables.

4.2.2. Reasons for Not Measuring Change Management

For twenty-two contributors, measuring change is not useful or possible for the following reasons:

- Difficult and too time-consuming.

- Political—it seems that when a change was been decided, it is by political decree that it must be a success (e.g., outsourcing to China), so there is no interest in measuring the effects.

- My organization does not measure the effectiveness of a change management process... [or] routinely measure change effectiveness in a quantifiable manner.

- There are no formal measures of change effectiveness.

- We are attempting to find a better way to track all phases, but not really in a position to formally do this, yet.

- We are not exact in our measuring...just beginning to manage this process. We measure these [changes] but do not attribute success to the effectiveness of a change management process.

- We are in a regulated business.

4.3. What Measures Should We Select?

It can be difficult to empirically explore if your change is working for the good of the organization:

- In a large organization, there is a continual emphasis on ROI. I believe this is a mistaken emphasis on the wrong things…however, change is important, if also hard to believe in and make right decisions about.

- The change management process is measured by data, and the impact on employees' morale and motivation isn't taken into consideration.

- It would be nice to have predictive metrics. We still use past-performance metrics.

- To do it right is a huge waste of time for most change efforts. You could spend the time tracking to move forward. Only large firms have the luxury and cash flow to contemplate their navels or everything—the rest of us have to work.

Change Metrics Selection Criteria

Many contributors offered criteria they used when it comes to selecting what metrics to use; here's a sampling:

- **Assess the impact of change**
- **Project management improvements**
- **Improve budgeting and influence forecasts for future changes**
- **Track transactional costs before/after**
- **Employee satisfaction**
- **Customer satisfaction**
- **Turns the soft stuff around culture change into hard business results**
- **Gauge the adoption time**
- **Performance enhancement**
- **Enhanced capacity for co-creation of new potential**

Here are some of the metrics contributors use to track and manage change.

Non-Employee Metrics	
Financial	**Marketing**
Cash flow and working capital	Public response
Market share	Needs met, a new set of customers located
Sales	Collaboration, including with suppliers
Increased throughput	Market acceptance
Sales of new programs	Market penetration

Employee Metrics	
Affective Metrics	**Effective Metrics**
Relationship capital	Performance improvement
Morale or satisfaction	Absenteeism
Reduced change resistance	Loyalty, retention, or attrition
Empathy or confidence	Understanding the change
Engagement or participation	Behavior change
Commitment to change or adoption	Talent development

TABLE 1: CONTRIBUTORS' NONEMPLOYEE METRICS

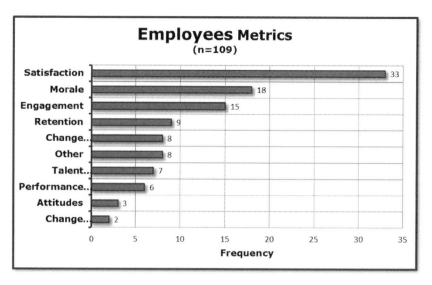

CHART 8: EMPLOYEES METRICS

4.4. How Do Better Metrics Help Gain and Retain Market Share?

It is surprising that there are so few comments relating to the connection between measuring change management and its impact on sales and marketing. This is not to say there is little measurement, but that there is little focus on correlating change management efforts with these two important areas of the business.

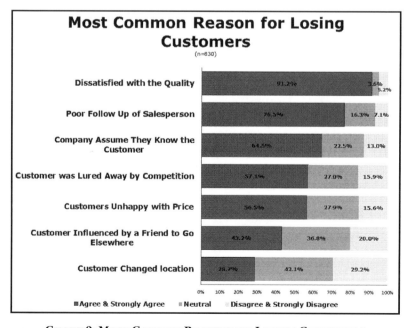

CHART 9: MOST COMMON REASON FOR LOSING CUSTOMERS

Those that did comment, though, saw a direct connection, such as the following:

- Becoming a stronger competitor

- Providing an opportunity for new avenues

- Gaining market share and staying ahead in the game

- Making the company more secure within the market

- Positioning us a leaders in our field

- Brand respected by peer companies with greater visibility and pricing premium commanded for the flagship products

- Builds customer loyalty

- Brand enhancement

The seriousness of these ratings is that many studies show that it costs six times more to get a new customer than it does to keep an existing one. Acquiring new customers is costly, and in many cases the money earned on the first sale doesn't even cover the acquisition costs.

If you look at the top three reasons for losing customers—poor quality, follow-up, and customer knowledge—and compare them with the change metrics used, you would think you were looking at two different universes. Look at the charts above: Where do you see customer-related change metrics?

These last three charts have an uncomfortable resonance with the lack of customer focus we see in other parts of this report. Change and competitive advantage are unequally yoked. Change drives, while competitive advantage is an apparent afterthought.

Nevertheless, many see that metrics play a crucial role in decision-making.

4.5. How Do Metrics Inform Decision-Making?

Other selection criteria of effective change metrics commented on was their impact on decision-making:

- Take stock, pause, get a sense of where you are in any given time during change…and look at the choices you have for what's next.

- Know how to logically prioritize the placement of resources, depending upon the ROI.

- Help maintain focus and meet long-term goals.

- Provide feedback of new changes, so we have early options to change our strategy.

- Stimulates proactivity and realigns with the strategic choices made.

4.6. Was It Worth It? Did We Get the ROI We Were Looking For?

This section gives the reader a sense of contributor's mind-set when it comes to answering the difficult question *Was it worth it?*

- We think [change metrics'] value is to put measurement into its messy context and remind us of what we really need to measure.

For leaders to answer this question, it helps to think of what may be on the minds of those they lead. Leaders' comments reflect not only their concerns as managers but also the concerns of those they serve and need to sustain implemented change.

The reader will get a sense of the emotional as well as the rational factors at work: as someone put it, "knowing when [we] have successfully crossed the finish line without losing our blood and soul." The following comments address four different aspects of change metrics.

4.6.1. ROI

- Did we make the right investment?

- How much have we changed?

- How much do we still need to change?

- How does the ROI we got compare with the open market?

4.6.2. Sustainability
- How sure are we that the change is embedded and sustainable?

- Is the change really for the good or better in the long run?

4.6.3. Corporate Growth
- What added value has been created?

- How well did we achieve our business case?

- How much follow-up will be needed over successive years?

- How are the sales indicators relating to keeping and growing customer revenues?

- How well are reimbursements growing due to [customer] satisfaction?

- What is the relationship between our goals and how they are supported by the change?

- How much profitability did we make for our customers, our business, and employees?

- What worked in the market (and what didn't)?

4.6.4. Change Success
- Has the change produced an outcome that was desired and meets the goals we set out with?

- What are the links between change outcomes and the vision for change?

- What is the relationship between actions and investment, and results achieved?

- What value did change management add?

- Was the change worth executing?

- To what extent did we reach our intended audience?

- Did we really make a difference?

  ➢ Was this is the correct change, or
  ➢ Was the old way of working was better?

4.7. What Can We Learn from Using Change Metrics?

Many experts in organizational learning—such as Gregory Bateson, Peter Senge, Andrew Pettigrew, and Richard Whipp—found a strong relationship between learning and competitiveness. Contributors reflect this in their comments on the crucial interplay of learning and the following abilities:

- Course-adjust quickly when specific metrics change

- Distill one project's lessons to improve future performance

- Identify how the learning process is defined and impacted

- The importance of understanding pragmatic and competitive learning

This next section looks at learning from two perspectives: the first is what questions people have when change is under way; the second, what has been learned for next time.

What Contributors Want Metrics to Help Answer

- How's it working? How's it not working?
- Where are we now? How far have we got to go?
- How well your process is working?
- How do we channel resources better?
- How fast is it working?
- How much are we saving? Time?
- What's urgent, and what is not?
- How much are we improving customer satisfaction?
- How much has to be re-worked?

4.7.1. Making Quick Course Adjustments—Learning as You Go

Contributors also focused on the following:

- Continuous learning and growth in the ever-competitive world

- Implementing lessons learned, so change becomes less feared

- Improving the approach to change

- *Using historical data to inform future changes*

For many, data helps supporting any efforts that are different from the past. It creates a new baseline and clear path for the next change. The change-management process is improved by learning from past changes and relating them to your goals for the current process.

Contributors specifically mentioned learning

- Success and, more importantly, from failure;

- About the organization and its relevance to the community;

- What was gained that can motivate for the next change;

- How change-related failures occurred and how to avoid them in the future;

- How the audience responded versus what was predicted; and

- What best practice should be shared, including

- What learnings should be accumulated for next time,

- How we can develop best practices, leaders, and teams, and

- How to reduce the learning curve once a change is implemented.

4.8. What Works, and What Doesn't?

The large number of failed projects indicates ineffective change management. Clearly, the ability to track what's working and what's not is crucial, according to the 212 comments we received.

Tracking teaches the organization how to retool change-management processes for more effective results. Reviewing the effectiveness of change-management processes allows us the opportunity to see what works and what doesn't as well as to push the envelope further to achieve additional success in the areas targeted.

The largest comments category was finding organizational gaps and needs. In addition, the ability to adjust in midcourse attracted more comments:

- An adjustment in the way the business is being driven…ensures that any adverse changes are picked up quickly and addressed.

- Are we moving in the right direction to meet the requirements of the client and marketplace we are serving?

- Having a target…forces focus on achieving it. If your measurements say you haven't achieved your target, then we know we need to adjust something we're doing.

Many contributors emphasized the importance of metrics to stimulate continual tweaking along the way. These midcourse corrections are needed to do the following:

- Take advantage of lessons learned

- Recalibrate strategy...processes

- Stop spending more money if not effective

- Adapt to ensure that actual benefits are realized and not just meeting budget

- Fine-tune along the way to see if you are indeed accomplishing your goals identify address issues early

- Keep on the correct pathway or process and meet milestones

- Change your approach to emerging markets and take decisions before it's too late.

4.9. Learning for Next Time

How often is a postmortem done to improve the next project? We don't know this from contributors, but we do know what they see as valuable outcomes from such a process and the burden it places on the metrics used. Here are some of their questions:

- How successful was the process?

- What was the measurable improvement and value added?

- What variables caused the best results?

- Did we make a positive difference?

- Did the process do make things worse?

- What was ineffective? How do we avoid going down that same path again and again?

- Was the strategy right?

- To what extent did the change occur for the right reasons and outcomes?

- What should we improve next time?

- What aspects of change made the most impact?

- What exactly worked best in terms of productivity/profitability?

4.10. What Does It Take to Adjust and Navigate around Change?

Focus on the snags and pocket vetoes that are slowing the change process, and know where the change process has been adopted and to what degree. Then you can do the following:

- Assure the best use of resources

- Ensure the adjustment is not just change for change's sake

- Control the possible chaos in change more effectively

- Coordinate within the organization

- Avoid confusion and misleading actions

- Understand the sources of resistance

- Remove barriers to change

Our final point in this section is to ensure the company's agility to modify or even change course. Many contributors commented on the need to know how to navigate during change's often-stormy times.

4.11. How Can Change Metrics Help Align Our People?

Many contributors are concerned about how to get people in agreement; their comments fall into five categories:

- Culture

- Confidence

- Engagement

- Satisfaction

- Performance

4.11.1. Culture

The benefits of measuring cultural alignment are clear to many contributors:

- Alignment of human and financial resources within the organization.

- Team unity/alignment.

- Benefits seen in everyday interactions; greater stability in individuals' working (fires are gone)

Learning, problem solving, and decision-making were all referenced in contributors' comments that they said lead to:

- **Process improvement**
- **More streamlined business**
- **More business**
- **Consistent performance**
- **Increased productivity**
- **Cost reduction**
- **Continuous improvement**
- **Doing the right things, right**
- **More innovation and creativity**
- **Avoiding future failures**

- Creating a like-mindedness: one voice, with similar goals and objectives…agreement between the lower staff and the upper management thus creates more customer satisfaction, increasing the firm's profitability.

- Staff respond positively to the change and that there are limited staff casualties.

- Staff retention, increased productivity, less rework (increased quality), happier customers, better reputation of company

- Confident and able employees and improved relations with trade unions and regulators

- Cooperation

4.11.2. Confidence

Demonstrating movement using credible measures that leaders act on builds people's confidence. Contributors cite that when the change road map is being followed, it gives a continuing sense of job security and retention. It seems that transparent sharing and participation in the process sets the tone for future efforts with, with "staff feeling they belong in a cause and their input is highly regarded by management."

Additionally, employees feel valued and less resistant when anecdotal evidence is gathered about their experiences during a change process, and they see that it was worth it. It then fosters more positive attitudes and productivity. Overall these contributors see the value in using such metrics:

- Minimizing resistance or doubt, about accepting change

- Seeing the benefits in terms that mean something to the organization

- Developing faster

- Building confidence going into the next change

- Supporting excellence and motivation in the organization

4.11.3. Engagement

Another area for some was the way that measured and transparent change increased employee's engagement and self-belief.

- Members know they are an active part of an evolving organization deeply interested in their needs.

Also, using metrics as the basis for involving people helped in management decision-making processes and lowered attrition levels in the talent pool.

- Working closely with each employee that reports to you builds world-class skills and behaviors.

4.11.4. Satisfaction

- Staff are happy + business is happy = profitability without headaches.

- When managers, stakeholders, and staff receive reports of objectively measured success, good news spreads quickly. Sharing in the celebration in achieving successful change builds esprit de corps. The importance for these contributors is as follows:

- When all levels know that their behaviors are contributing to successful change management, then good things happen.

- Employee-expressed satisfaction with the new method or change then rises, which creates better morale, loyalty, and change compliance.

4.12. How Can Metrics Help Us Improve What We Do?

Many contributors commented on using change metrics to help improve people's performance, especially when people receive feedback from internal and external stakeholders. Employees then feel part of the company and want to work together to stretch and adjust.

Contributors cite the following benefits:

- Motivation

- Customer responsiveness

- Cooperation

- Participation

- Productivity

- Stability and growth

- Build excellence

- Retention

Overall change progress develops learning, improved organizational effectiveness, and efficiency. It is especially powerful when concerns are acknowledged. This condition then builds:

- More confidence and willingness to adopt change…An opportunity to reflect and capture wisdom for the next change process.

Learning, problem-solving, and decision-making were all referenced in contributors' comments; they said these three tactics led to the following:

- Process improvement

- More streamlined business

- More business

- Consistent performance

- Increased productivity

- Cost reduction

- Continuous improvement

- Doing the right things, right

- More innovation and creativity

- Avoiding future failures

4.13. How Can Metrics Help Us Sell Change?

For the contributors, an important benefit of change metrics is showing that change is working and can work in the future. Here's what they said change metrics can do:

- Set a precedent to demonstrate to the board and internal employees that a goal properly executed can achieve a mutually desirable outcome

- Enhance senior management's commitment to change

- Show how the change-management plan is working regarding sales results tied to the business plan

- Show how it is meeting business objectives

- Show how investing in change correlates with productivity and profitability

- Reveal hard facts on what can be improved from important stakeholders.

- Demonstrate financial prudence, fiduciary responsibility, and extent of the improvement resulting from the change

- Make it easier to get management to invest

- Allow reporting of progress

- Create support for future change

- Justify new change efforts in the future

- Keep leaders, managers, and change agents engaged in process

- Keep the accountants happy

All these benefits suggest a credible and objective change story. The contributors' focus is on gaining sufficient resources and attention to do change management properly the next time.

- [There is a] need for concrete information to discuss with all stakeholders and part of the change-response-change process.

- Evaluation tells the best story of how to channel resources in the short and long run. Without evaluation, there isn't a clear indication of what works and what does not work.

Essential to effective change management is relaying change impacts factually to employees, so they stay connected to establishing and embedding change. This is a key part of proving that the change is embedded and sustainable.

4.14. Show the Change, Sell the Change

Contributors place great emphasis on demonstrating the rate of change and the relationship with their organization's strategy and financial results. As one contributor commented,

- Demonstrating the ability to change and be agile builds trust and stability [for] customers.

Some say this is obvious, but here's the kicker: If this is common sense, why is there so little common practice? Yes, we all recognize the need for measurement, yet how often do we think about these issues when planning change and how to reliably collect and analyze the data? Apparently 30 percent of respondents' organizations don't measure change, or they don't know if they do.

Conversely, here are some comments on the benefits of using metrics to sell change:

- Creating an opportunity for the development of best practices, leadership, and team development.

- Creating trust in the organization and cultural acceptance of a new way of thinking.

- Showing how we implemented [change] without negatively affecting the day-to-day business and how effectiveness is maintained or even improved.

- Motivation and employee performance increases when staff feel supported and understand the change process.

- Keeping us focused on the proper direction for our customers.

Change measurement covers a daunting array of possibilities. Certainly these more than seven hundred commentators attest to that. They echo what many experts say about change leaders' skill in devising meaningful and credible frameworks for managing change.

The challenge many face is to position change measurement as a blend of lagging and leading indicators. Lagging indicators keep score, and leading indicators alert you to the direction and pace of change. The trap for both the enthusiastic novice and the jaded professional is the seduction of the easy-to-measure. This is especially true when they are too reliant on those lagging metrics currently in use, which are difficult to correlate with behavioral, cultural, and societal issues. This is also doubly challenging when trying to get leaders' agreement to subjective metrics—before the change is implemented.

Even when agreement on metrics is reached, the next challenge is creating greater transparency through the organization so that they are used to create and sustain change momentum. These issues are covered in detail in section 7.

Now go to the next page and see if this section's actions points can help you improve your change metrics and increase your chances of a smoother transition and successful change outcomes.

4.15. Questionnaire: What Questions Do Change Metrics Need to Answer?

These next tables capture contributor questions they posed in their comments. If these questions are important, then they will foster the appropriate metrics.

Please go through and rate your organization's ability to provide metrics against those items you rate as important. There are three sections of questions:

- Navigating during a change

- Reviewing a change

- Planning the next change

Contributor Questions That Change Metrics Need to Answer

Navigating During Change		How well do your change metrics help? (5 = very well, 1=not at all)				
		1	2	3	4	5
NC 1	Where are we?					
NC 2	How far have we gotten?					
NC3	What's left to be done?					
NC4	Are we going in the right direction?					
NC5	Where are we, after making changes?					
NC6	How well is the change process working?					
NC7	How do we channel resources better?					
NC 8	How fast is it working?					
NC 9	How much are we saving?					
NC 10	What's urgent, and what is not?					
NC 11	How much is customer satisfaction improving?					
NC 12	How much has to be reworked?					
	Navigating a Change Totals					

Contributor Questions That Change Metrics Need to Answer						
Reviewing Change	How well do your change metrics help? (5 = very well, 1=not at all)					
		1	2	3	4	5
RC1	What was the measurable improvement and value added?					
RC2	What aspects of change made the most impact? How much do we still need to change?					
RC3	To what extent did we reach our intended audience?					
RC4	What was ineffective? How do we avoid going down that same path again and again?					
RC5	Is the change really for the good, or better, in the long run?					
RC6	How sure are we that the change is embedded and sustainable?					
RC7	How much follow-up will be needed over successive years?					
RC8	How are revenues growing due to customer satisfaction?					
RC9	How much profitability did we make for our customers, business, and employees?					

Contributor Questions That Change Metrics Need to Answer

	Reviewing Change	How well do your change metrics help? (5 = very well, 1=not at all)				
		1	2	3	4	5
RC10	What are the links between change outcomes and the vision for change?					
RC11	Was the old way of doing things working better?					
RC12	How much more confidence and willingness to adopt change has been achieved?					
RC13	What value did change management add? Was the change worth executing? Did we make the right investment?					
RC14	What new changes need to be added?					
	Reviewing Change Totals					

Contributor Questions That Change Metrics Need to Answer						
Planning the Next Change		**How well do your change metrics help? (5 = very well, 1=not all)**				
		1	2	3	4	5
PC1	What variables and dependencies need to be considered?					
PC2	What strengths do we want to capitalize?					
PC3	What can be repeated in the future?					
PC4	What changes in terms of trends and needs in the market need to be considered?					
PC5	What strengths do we want to capitalize?					
PC6	What pitfalls do we want to avoid?					
PC7	What baseline do we need for the next time?					
PC8	What risks are we prepared to take?					
PC9	What issues do we need to plan for?					
PC10	How fast can we implement?					
Planning the Next Change Totals						

TABLE 2: CONTRIBUTORS' QUESTIONS THAT CHANGE METRICS NEED TO ANSWER

4.16. Action Points 3: Developing More Effective Change Metrics

What's the Difference between Leading and Lagging Metrics?

When developing a change scorecard, we suggest that you use a balance of leading and lagging indicators.

The idea is that without leading indicators, you will not know how your outcomes will be achieved, nor will you have any early warnings about being off track toward achieving your change goals.

Similarly, with only lagging indicators, you risk focusing on short-term performance, at the expense of achieving broader change outcomes: for example, achieving cost-saving goals at the expense of building a competitively agile culture.

Leading indicators enable you to take preemptive actions to improve your chances of successful change.

(Adapted from Ian J. Seath, Simply Improvement*)*

Action Points 3: Developing More Effective Change Metrics

Protocol
Three themes were referenced in contributor comments about change metrics and how to test their overall effectiveness.

- How well do your change metrics accelerate learning, problem-solving, and decision-making?

Establish Your Change Scorecard
It is strongly suggested that you go through this process with your leadership team and key stakeholders. (See section 7 for more details.)

- Review the table Contributor Questions.
- Agree on those questions your team need to answer when you are doing the following:
  - ➢ Navigating a change
  - ➢ Reviewing a change
  - ➢ Planning the next change
- What current metrics could be put to good use?
- How well do they cover the risks of *losing customers* through poor-quality sales follow-up during the change process?
- How well do they inform you that the organization is reducing assumptions about customers' view of the change and how the change responds to their needs?
- To what extent do your selected metrics allow you to preempt or least respond quickly to competitors
- How well do these metrics allow you to gauge and track employee stress around the change?
- To what extent will your metrics allow you to respond quickly and effectively to employee stress before it hardens their change resistance?

And finally,

How well does your scorecard help you sell this and subsequent changes?

Section 5: How Can Implementing Change Gain Competitive Advantage?

Even after thirty years, the connections between change management and gaining competitive advantage are not well articulated. The discrepancies between commitments to change and actual competitive behavior are a major factor in the seemingly intractable proportion of change initiative failures—still at 60 percent.

Getting *beyond imitators* relies on understanding and measuring behavior that distinguishes competitive behavior from other activities.

A key area of using change management to gain competitive advantage is effective learning. Competitive research by people like Pettigrew & Whipp[9] and Senge[10] repeatedly find that effective learning both individually and collectively is central to sustained success. As one contributor said,

- Learning keeps us ahead of the competition by getting us closer to selected customers to gather competitive intelligence.

This market and customer sensing of trends and tactics enable sense-making to improve competitive tactics.

Learning is one of five areas in which we analyzed contributor comments on connecting the dots between managed change and competitiveness. This enables us to propose a practical assessment tool for readers to assess their own organization.

Overall, contributors comment that managing change for competitive success is a continuous process that is dynamic and nonlinear. For them it's systemic, repetitive, and uncertain.

---

9 "Creating Competitive Success Out of Uncertainty," based on Nick Anderson's master's thesis reflects Pettigrew and Whipp's research and book *Managing Change for Competitive Success.(1996)*
10 *The Fifth Discipline* by Peter M. Senge (1997).

Here are two comments that capture contributors' perspective:

- Understanding who you are as an organization, where you are going, and how you are going to get there will give you advantage.

- Change ensures you are ahead of the competition...Response to changing markets must be immediate.

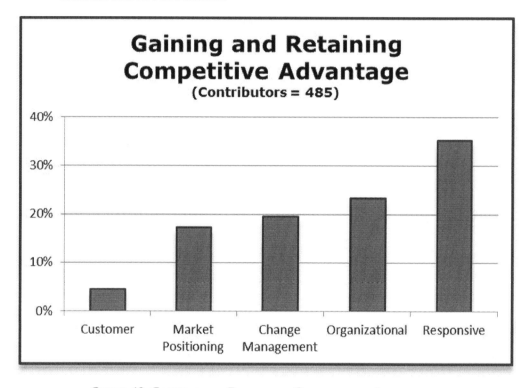

CHART 10: GAINING AND RETAINING COMPETITIVE ADVANTAGE

Look at the above chart. It shows contributors' focuses of on five main categories are listed below:

- Responsiveness—speed, staying ahead, agility, learning, awareness

- Organizational—leadership, alignment, communication, engagement, focus, culture, people

- Change management—change, planning, measurement

- Marketing positioning—marketing, product, improve, innovate, research

- Customer-changing needs, strategies, decision making

What strikes you about these leaders, managers, and consultants' focus? Once again we see little explicit focus on the customer. This seems to correlate with contributors' ratings of why they lose business:

- Poor quality—91.2 percent

- Poor follow-up by salespeople—76.5 percent

- Assuming they know the customer—64.5 percent

Ask yourself, What would be your order of comments in this area? We would argue that comments which explicitly mention the customer and our partners should be first.

After reading contributor comments on the above issues, look at how these contributors discriminate between the *thriving* and just *surviving* organization in section 6. That section is set up to give you rating scales based on contributor comments from which you can select those that are relevant and most valuable to poll your people or clients. We would ask that you give us feedback on those you choose.

This first section covers the following:

Contributors' answers to the question - How Can Implementing Change Gain and retain Competitive Advantage? are listed in descending order, from first to last:

- Change as a competitive weapon

- Competitive agility—anytime, anywhere, on anything

- Competitive learning and training

- Staying ahead

- Are people really your first priority?

- Markets and marketing

- Is the customer really king?

- Culture—Is This Your Secret Ingredient?

- What Is the Role of Innovation?

5.1. Change as a Competitive Weapon

It is interesting to look at people's answers to why change can be a competitive advantage.

- Change is competitive advantage for those who do it well.

- Change readiness allows
a company to stay ahead
of the curve and to be
in a position to react to
market influences. It allows
organizations to go for
new technology, better
performance, customer
satisfaction, and lower costs.

  > - **When change is done well, it creates opportunity and competitive advantage as the natural result.**
  > - **Well-executed change effectively means less disruption and "taxes paid" in resistance and even "dividends" earned from positively embracing the unknown.**

- Organizations that predict
and adapt to changing
circumstances are more
likely to lead change and move ahead of those who resist or ignore it.

- [People] have to be change-ready. Just like [other] people, if we don't change, we don't continue.

- Reactive change is inefficient and frustrating…. Proactive change… can happen at a reasonable and understandable pace, resulting in more collaboration from people…then people get to the stage of never stopping looking for next thing to do.

When organizations change only when forced to, change is more expensive, and organizations will be lagging behind leaders. For many, implementing change should be as natural as selling and be an everyday activity.

5.1.1. When Change is a Constant

Contributors commented further on long-term change management:

- Once change is an accepted fact, people always have their innovative and creative hats on, seeking new ways to improve outcomes, thus creating an opening for their organization to become an industry leader. When they embrace it, love it, and don't feel threatened by it, you can grow and market it! Improved knowledge, process, and expertise follows. It means you stay competitive.

- Accepting change frees up people to look at the bigger competitive picture. Then this forms the basis for creating a robust culture that is adaptable and high-performing. Crucially, when this capability is leveraged with your customers and you collaborate in changing, you can competitively inoculate yourself.

The critical dynamic is that people's comfort level with change is directly proportional to their competitiveness.

In summary, if you create an involvement-centered change culture, you can adapt faster competitively to market forces and beat the competition to the punch.

5.1.2. When is a Change to Your Competitive Advantage, and When Isn't It?

Contributors offer counterweights to change as a competitive weapon with cautions of *change for change's sake.* They see many companies who don't get it. As one person wrote,

- Sometimes reinvigorating old processes has merit too. Many times because we are going through so much change now, excellence in workmanship and making the most technologically advanced products for a fair price is better than making goods that are cheap.

Several others caution that change is effective only when it's warranted. Changing too often is counterproductive if it does not support your strategic objectives.

Here's a summary of contributors' suggested criteria:

Does the change you are considering do the following?
- Differentiate your company on its ability to change and make it harder for others to copy

- Develop and help the business succeed

- Improve business that gives you an advantage

- Minimize the negative impact on the business

- Enable a course correction to meet your goals

- Have a sound objective and plan to achieve competitive advantage (or is this change for change's sake?)

- Drive change in your industry

- Prevent your competitor from seizing the initiative (In the long run, it's usually is more expensive to copy innovation)

- Allow you enough time for your people to grow, learn, and adapt (before moving on to next large-scale change)

When they do meet these criteria, then contributors' thoughts turn to setting up for success.

5.1.3. Being First: Outpacing the Competition
Speed emerged as contributors' first priority: changing or responding to business opportunities quicker than competitors do. Bringing new products to market quickly is a typical example. This is seen as the prerequisite to thriving in today's global environment. Without keeping up with the changing environment, many say they will fall behind and fail.

- Innovation is needed, but implementation speed is more important to get maximum adoption.

- Be proactive: don't just react to what's going on in [your] environment—try to shape it.

- For contributors, quick responses to changes in markets, new competitors, and new opportunities are crucial.

- Changing swiftly and without hassle allows organizations to thrive in constantly changing markets while giving them competitive advantage. Those who adapt fastest gain competitive advantage. For many, implementing change better, earlier, and faster means you have the luxury of proactive action and can dictate change to your competitors.

- In practical terms it means reducing your time-to-market from first identifying the opportunity to implement change.

Customer and market perceptions change when you implement better and faster. Several comments on the impact of better and faster change follow:

- Recognition as leaders within the industry

- Being established as innovators and cooperative with customers

- Being seen as early adopters who can get ahead of curve

- Reaping benefits of a well-calculated risk

- Faster ROI and improved bottom line

- Shortened adaptation time

Faster change also means the following:

- Bigger competitive advantages.

- More adopters of your new technology, services, concepts, and so on.

- Learning something new to gain quicker return on investment.

- Less resistance (to change), thus taking advantage of new opportunities and outpacing the competition.

- Greater impact than competitors have.

- Adapting to market changes.

- Being first to change means you get the contract.

5.2. Competitive Agility—Anytime, Anywhere, On Anything

For some contributors, change agility is more important than all other factors. Adaptability to change, anytime, anywhere, and on anything can be seen as stable and helps build integrity and customers' trust. Being nimble and adaptable to market requirements creates opportunities for early market entry. Delivering such agility and flexibility internally drives innovation externally.

Agility is change-embracing and develops preemptive abilities. Agile companies are more likely to initiate change and gain competitive advantage over larger, slower-moving corporations.

Agility allows a company to do business and not spend time reacting to problems and issues. Embracing agility, rather than striving to maintain the status quo, means you are more likely to deliver customer value.

It follows, for many contributors, that agility leads to deeper relationships internally and customers. This is a key driver for sustained growth. The other valuable outcomes are that agility tends to do the following:

- Be unique and hard to duplicate

- Can correct bad practices more quickly

- Have a better chance of being more profitable than are less responsive competitors

- Be dynamic and successfully make adjustments to maintain profitability

- More responsiveness to customers, markets, and new opportunities

As one person said,

- For one thing, your competitor has to reckon with a "moving target," which is always more difficult to compete with! Keep an eye on what is happening in the market, and be ready to change. Preparedness to turn on a dime is the ability to adapt to and implement change easily.

It follows that agile companies have change processes and policies that can be activated with ease.

5.2.1. Becoming Agile

Many contributors commented on how to become more agile:

- Take small steps toward great results.

- Develop change as a core competency.

- Adapt core competencies as environmental forces dictate.

- Don't have frozen protocols…and change should not be a radical departure, it's a way of life…adapting…to be of greater service to customers—it's not about us: it's about those we serve.

- Prepare to adapt to new challenges and face change as opportunity.

- Listen to customers and the market to spot opportunities and work toward them together.

- Create a sense of company ownership that is inclusive.

- Develop processes that move and adapt faster, more efficiently, and [more] effectively than the competition

- In our global economy, agility is what determines a long-term future for an organization. Take a look at Blockbuster; [they] are closing because NetFlix came along [and] introduced a better way while [Blockbuster] stayed the same.

Contributors focus on difficult-to-imitate strategies that are meaningful to customers by doing the following:

- Doing things differently [than] the competition

- Researching current customer demands [that] are key to sustaining an advantage

- Changing in a way that capitalizes on people's talents and strengths that support customer needs

- Successful organizations continuously work on:

  ➢ Enhanced processes,

  ➢ Better efficiencies,

  ➢ Improved cost-benefits,

  ➢ Better predictability, and

  ➢ Better customer satisfaction/retention.

- Smarter working to stay more effective and better motivated

- Get ahead of game

- Maintain leadership position

- Stay constantly on top of the market

- Keep innovating

5.3. Preparing People for Change

- Start educating people about what change management is (and how it contributes to competitive advantage). Most people don't understand their role and responsibilities.

Contributors stress the need to train and develop people to consistently understand customers and coworkers' changing needs by doing the following:

- Developing technological, efficiency, and service skills

- Staying current

- Sharing best practices interactively and electronically

- Awareness of both inside and outside [their] field

- Sharing results, information, and knowledge

- Being collaboratively creative

- Developing the willingness and skills to listen to customers

- Facilitating and listening to feedback

- Learning how to change so when you need to, you can

- Gaining insights and engaging the entire organization in the change process.

- Staying humble, teachable, and accountable

5.3.1. Learning With and From Customers

- Gathering and listening to customer ideas, needs, and wants can elevate brand awareness and loyalty.

If a company listens to employees' ideas, needs, and wants, it fosters positive attitudes and a more productive environment. Then the company can share process changes and benefits with key customers while staying alert to what works and what doesn't.

5.4. Staying Ahead

Contributors make distinctions between speed, agility, and staying ahead. For them, getting to the front is one thing, but staying in the lead is another. Let's see what they said.

- Maintain a one-step-ahead concept while becoming more cost effective (internally and externally).

- See change as a positive process to improve something already good rather than [as] a response to deficiency.

- Get to the cutting edge and stay there.

- Get there first, and then move forward again—never be "me too."

- Stay up-to-date with strategies and processes to deliver [your] product or service in a manner that surpasses customer desires and needs, [which] makes it hard for those trying to catch you.

5.5. People—Your First Change Priority?

Many contributors talk of tensions between people's experience and how they would like to be treated during a change. Many cite poor leadership and the lack of respect for people as toxic factors in their organization's culture. On the positive side, several reflect the sentiments of this contributor:

- [Develop] change-management practices that keep staff engaged and positive in looking for possibilities and cost-effective processes.

As one person put it,

- People are actually very adaptive, and we change all the time. We just don't believe we do a good job at change, until someone helps us understand the reasons and results of change.... Successful leaders understand that people deal with change all the time, so if leaders can explain change in terms everyone understands and sees the benefit of…it will go better.

For many, it's about getting people's buy-in so that they own part of the process that will increase competitive advantage. It's striking that there is a theme of the individual. For these contributors, it's about *engaging individually*. As one person noted,

- It is important to communicate with each individual how the big picture relates to his or her specific job. If you can help them visualize where they are and where they need to be, most people will embrace change….Listen to people and respect their opinion; even if what is proposed cannot be done, it will tighten trust, and trust is key in change.

5.6. Markets and Marketing

For contributors, marketing comes down to seeing the current reality and trends honestly. This assessment then leads to developing assets that can produce what the market demands while constantly improving processes using any available technology.

5.6.1. Market Awareness (Sensing)

Several contributors referred to the importance of market and competitive awareness:

- Know your competitors and their strengths and weaknesses.

- Gauge the value for service delivered.

- Forecast future customer needs to develop benefits not previously seen.

- Forecast changes in markets, and foster innovation.

Based on this external sensing, you can then do the following:

- Identify and take advantage of new opportunities.

- Produce strong, clear messaging.

- Show the world you are keeping up.

- Build market share with new product development.

- Create new segments.

- Responsiveness to market changes will confer advantages over nonresponsive organizations.

5.7. Continuous Improvement (CI)

The implied link of continuous improvement (CI) with speed, agility, and staying ahead is a legitimate connection. Many contributors' earlier comments imply continuous improvement. The curiosity here is the scarcity of comments referencing the quality movement mantras like —

Deming, Six Sigma, Kaisen, and TQM (Total Quality Management)—and how they link to managing change for competitive success.

Here's a synopsis of comments on continuous improvement.

- Manage all change as a project, track change, measure success/failure, and, most importantly, learn from your mistakes. You can then sustain what works and change what doesn't. Then continuously assess opportunity for change and plan for it.

- Reduce time to drive change. Increase urgency—inspire people to move; make objectives real and relevant.

- Continuous improvement reduced turnaround time, cost advantage, and basically made our organization agile.

Few people made explicit links between continuous improvement and change management. Yes, there were comments on developing best practices and references to the following:

- Process and services quality

- Productivity and efficiency made "lean"

- Cutting overhead

- Removing wasteful and unproductive processes

- Not wasting time or resources

- Reengineering systems and processes

- Periodic process evaluation and improvement

- Documenting processes and results to spread success and including customers

- Maximizing intellectual capital

- Kaizen events (rapid improvement events involving key people in and around process of focus)

- Obtain (in ISO-9001:2008 terms) effective and efficient IT tools, procedures, (technology) knowledge, and so on.

5.8. Is the Customer Really King?

We all experience leaders' exhortations to "*focus on the customer*" and "*develop customer value*"; and of course we've heard countless times that "*the customer is king.*"

So, why is customer focus ranked sixth in comments on managing change for competitive advantage?

As one contributor put it,

- Many claim that their customers are important. But what kind of experience are they providing for customers with their products, services, communications, and interactions? How are customers really treated? The answer is, often badly, despite all protestations to the contrary. Think of unusable websites, uninspiring campaigns, or unresponsive customer service.

There is no doubt what people write about reflects their focus, language, and cultural predilections. So how do we reconcile all tools, techniques, and literature on sales and marketing to the apparent lack of focus on the customer?

Here's a flavor of those comments specifically referencing the customer:

- Recognize that services and products do not but solutions do solve customer problems. This should stimulate innovation, which gives a better view of your customer.

- Have a formal change process that gives customers reassurance.

5.9. Listen to Your Customer

Our synopsis of customer-centered comments continues, with a focus on *listening*.

- Listen better to the VOC (Voice of the Customer); act faster on things that are important to them.

- Get closer to customers and the market, then build competitive knowledge of customer strengths and weaknesses.

- Recognize what customers want or need and study/implement the best ways of providing for those wants and needs.

- Your users or frontline people actually know what your offerings should consist of.

- The best input about product or service desires comes from users of those products and services.

- Question your customer base as to what they really want or need to see in your product or service.

5.9.1. Managing Change for Competitive Advantage with Customers

Earlier we outlined the criteria for deciding to change or improve. The strongest case to change is covered by one contributor:

- If you decide to change because your customers really wanted it *and* it brings value to the end-user, then it will always drive a competitive advantage…. It's about staying relevant to those you serve.

Proactively implementing change *with* customers creates or maintains competitive advantages:

- Making change to meet customer needs first!

- Engaging customer input at an early stage, so that trends and requirements are integrated into the new business model before your competitors

- Depending upon the change, include your customers in communiqués and change set-up.

- Implementing positive changes and systems helps improve the customer experience.

- Making sure customers are aware and are pleased with the change.

- Ensure the least amount of change to customer organization.

5.10. Culture—The Secret Ingredient?

Here's what contributors said about the relationship between *culture, change,* and *competitive advantage.* Here's a typical comment on culture and competitive change management:

- Making and embracing change is part of…successful corporate culture. If people are constantly changing, they are more likely to embrace change. Those [companies] that thrive on change are flexible and quick to realize competitive benefits without losing momentum.

Here are some comments:

- Organization-wide change helps build a robust character. Being robust then becomes way of life. This can only happen through innovative implementation of change, which in turn results in an overall competitive advantage.

- Adapt to change quickly, and you will have tactical advantage over a company that is stagnant.

- An adaptive culture will more readily seize new opportunities and rarely cling to old practices and shrinking revenue channels.

- Organizational culture is important not only to members of the organization but also to its customers and stakeholders.

5.11. What Is the Role of Innovation?

That a company needs to improve its products and services regularly through innovation is a truism, but how many see that innovative change implementation plays a role in developing competitive strength?

5.11.1. Innovative Implementation of Change

Here contributors see competitive advantage in innovation to address issues such as

- Arming yourself to fight competition;

- Capitalizing on key advantages that may be identified earlier;

- Making sure that you are ahead of the competition;

- Delivering products to the customer quicker, cheaper, and with the best quality; and

- Developing new techniques to develop new business.

5.11.2. The Role of Innovation

Contributors comment on the constant need to innovate to ensure number one market position, and that can happen only through effective processes.

- Innovation should become a way of life. Companies like Bosch have three patents per day on average. Companies like CISCO are unique.

- Contributors suggested that each organization should create unique product or service that has competitive advantage across the industry and its verticals.

They see innovation as central to gaining competitive advantage. As one contributor suggested,

- Turn innovation into industry leadership and show that investment and calculated risk-taking leads to better organizations.

Others gave their reasoning of innovation's importance:

- Allowing things to be done better, faster, and cheaper.

- Eliminating activities altogether, thus releasing time and effort to make improvements and to increase profits.

- Developing new ways of doing things and being ahead of the pack can yield both bottom-line and top-line advantages.

- For example, watch how new technologies are improving customer experiences, and consider how your firm may be able to deliver similar benefits in your space.

- Bringing in new ways of working, applying technology, and refocusing the workforce.

- Streamlining and becoming more cost-effective.

Having more time for innovations builds customer loyalty:

- Innovation is used a lot, as if it is easy to do. Reality is that for most organizations, it is both hard and very costly. I think there is less successful innovation occurring than we talk about.

- *Any change that is inspired and expressed through innovation is always a competitive advantage over one that is enforced.*

5.12. What's Missing?

Areas of response to our questionnaire that surprised us were the lack of comments on rewards, incentives, and holding people accountable for changing. For example, there was only *one* comment that mentioned accountability:

- Make people accountable! Put your change goals into their annual performance review, and expect results.

Another area that people didn't comment on was the role of selection and recruitment:

- Seeking change-makers (where people, leaders, or ideas) always can give any company a competitive advantage.

- Get the right people in place with the right emotional commitment.

5.12.1. Stakeholder Importance

Contributors are clear on stakeholder roles. Here's the sort of things they stress:

- Prepare a change team around you that trusts each other. Ensure the team is balanced and avoid having too many people that are alike.

- Ensure that the right people are leading implementation of change and that they are truly on board.

They see that it is vital to involve stakeholders early in decision-making and planning while ensuring they are involved from end to end. Contributors report that this is the only way to ensure stakeholders' support and engagement, provided leaders follow through and keep encouraging them.

Others emphasize the importance of *cocreating change*. This takes engagement to a deeper level, where contributors advocate the following:

- Gather intelligence from all stakeholders.

- Engage them in the change process.

- Seek their input.

- Recognize their participation and celebrate their achievements.

- Keep all parties close and informed.

- Develop stakeholders as ambassadors of change.

For all people, contributors focus on keeping your human capital happy:

- Preparing individuals for their changing roles

- Continuous participation

- Ensuring people feel appreciated and listened to

- Encouraging people to develop out-of-the-box ideas and rewarding them for innovation, even when something doesn't work out

- Keeping them involved in the process and inviting ideas for improving your planning

- Ensuring that their needs are met (metaphysical, emotional, mental, and spiritual)

- Seeing things through various ideas of improvement from initiation to implementation

5.13. Action Points 4: Implementing Change to Gain Competitive Advantage—Questionnaire and Protocols

Contributors tell us that they initiate change every twelve months or less often. At least three drivers trigger these changes. In this environment, being clear about how to use limited resources to the best competitive advantage is essential. The following action points helps you think through implementing change as a competitive weapon.

Contributors' Questions on Implementing Change to Gain Competitive Advantage

The following questionnaire is based on 781 contributors' comments on implementing change to gain competitive advantage. It is designed to engage those involved in change leadership to select relevant questions and reach consensus on the following improvement areas.

1. Competitive Agility
2. Competitive Drivers
3. People's Change Readiness and Competitive Competence
4. The Customer Is King—Right?
5. Competitive Marketing and Market Awareness
6. Continuous Improvement
7. Creating the Competitively Requiring Environment

How well does your change rate?	Not well		Very well		
Competitive Agility	1	2	3	4	5
AG1 How well does this change improve your readiness take on new technology, improve performance and customer satisfaction, and lower costs?					
AG2 How well are you doing things differently from the competition (or are you just following the herd)?					
AG3 How well does your change capitalize on people's talents and strengths that support customer needs?					
AG4 How well are you set up to make quick responses to changes in markets, new competitors, and new opportunities?					
Totals					

Competitive Drivers						
How Well Does Your Change Rate?		Not well	Very well			
		1	2	3	4	5
CD1	How well do you do things differently than the competition?					
CD2	How well are you getting ahead of the competition?					
CD3	How well does this change help you stay ahead of the curve and in a position to react?					
CD4	How effectively are you maintaining a leadership position?					
CD5	How well does this change distinguish your company for its ability to change and make it harder for others to copy?					
CD6	What well will this change improve your ability to drive change in your industry?					
CD7	How well does this change prevent competitors (name them) from seizing the initiative?					
CD8	How well do you encourage and use competitive feedback from your customer-facing people?					
CD9	How well do you identify competitive strengths and weaknesses?					
CD10	How well are you attuned to users' feedback on your product or service, compared to the competition?					
	Totals					

People's Change Readiness and Competitive Competence

How Well Does Your Change Rate?		Not Well			Very Well	
		1	2	3	4	5
PPL1	How well do your people learn and change?					
PPL2	How well does this change help develop people's change readiness?					
PPL3	How well does this change increase collaboration across departments?					
PPL4	How well are you educating people about the links between change management and competitive advantage?					
PPL5	How well or thoroughly do you consider how much time you allow for your people to grow, learn, and adapt (before moving on to the next large-scale change)?					
PPL6	How well does your organization develop technological, efficiency, and customer service skills?					
PPL7	How well do your people stay current and up-to-date?					
PPL8	How well do your people interactively and electronically share best practices?					
PPL9	How well do your people network with those both inside and outside of your field?					

People's Change Readiness and Competitive Competence						
How Well Does Your Change Rate?		Not Well			Very Well	
		1	2	3	4	5
PPL10	How well do people share results, information, and knowledge?					
PPL11	How well do your people facilitate and listen to feedback from both their colleagues and their customers?					
	Totals					

The Customer Is King—Right?

	How Well Does Your Change Rate?	Not Well			Very Well	
		1	2	3	4	5
CS1	Overall, how well do you make proactive changes to meet customer needs before your competition does?					
CS2	How well do you engage customers to identify their needs and integrate these needs into change before your competitors do?					
CS3	How well do you listen to the VOC (voice of the customer) and act quickly on things that are important to them?					
CS4	How well do you establish and maintain closeness to customers and the market, compared to your competitors?					
CS5	How well are you researching current customer demands to gain a competitive advantage?					
CS6	To well are you gathering and listening to customer ideas, needs, and wants to elevate brand awareness and loyalty?					
CS7	How well do you gauge the value for service delivered?					
CS8	How well do you include your customers in communiqués and change set-up?					
CS9	How well do you implement changes and systems that help improve the customer experience?					
	Totals					

Competitive Marketing And Market Awareness

How Well Does Your Change Rate?	Not Well		Very Well		
	1	2	3	4	5
MA1 How well do you know your competitors—their strengths and weaknesses?					
MA2 How well do you forecast future customer needs and use these forecasted needs to develop new benefits?					
MA3 How well do you forecast market changes and use them to foster innovation?					
MA4 How well do your people identify and take advantage of new opportunities?					
MA5 How well do your marketing people produce strong, clear messaging?					
MA6 How well do you show the world that you are keeping up with your competition?					
MA7 How well have you established a track record for building market share and new segments through new product development?					
Totals					

Continuous Improvement					
How Well Does Your Change Rate?	**Not Well**			**Very Well**	
	1	**2**	**3**	**4**	**5**
CI1 How well does your process, services, quality, and evaluation work?					
CI2 How well do you maintain productivity and efficiency that is "lean"?					
CI3 How well do you obtain and retain quality certifications?* *Including ISO, SAS70, CQE, CQT, CRE, CQI, CQA, CMQ/OE, CSQE, CHA, CQIA, CSSBB, CBA, CCT, CQPA, CSSGB, CSGP, CMBB, effective and efficient IT tools, procedures, technology, knowledge, and so on.					
CI4 How well are you cutting overheads?					
CI5 How well are you removing waste and unproductive processes?					
CI6 How well are you engineering systems and processes?					
CI7 How well are you documenting processes and results to spread success, including to customers?					
CI8 How well are you maximizing our intellectual capital?					
Totals					

Creating The Competitively Required Environment						
How Well Does Your Change Rate?		Not Well			Very Well	
		1	2	3	4	5
CRE1	How well do you ensure that people understand their roles and responsibilities specific to this change?					
CRE2	How well do you hold people, managers, and leaders accountable for this specific change?					
CRE3	How well matched are peoples' accountabilities for your change goals and their annual performance reviews?					
CRE4	How well do you ensure that you have the right people in place, with the right emotional commitment to your change?					
CRE5	How well balanced is your change team? (Avoid having too many people who are alike).					
CRE6	How well prepared is your change team? And to what extent do they trust one another?					
CRE7	How well have you ensured that you have the right people leading your change implementation?					
	Totals					

TABLE 3: CONTRIBUTORS' QUESTIONS ON IMPLEMENTING
CHANGE TO GAIN COMPETITIVE ADVANTAGE

Action Points 4: Implementing Change to Gain Competitive Advantage

Based on your answers above, use the following questions to develop your plan for using change to your competitive advantage.

1. Market and Competitive Sensing
    - What do managers do at present to maintain awareness of your competitive environment?
    - How well do managers use this information to make more competitive decisions?
    - What should managers do to improve awareness and agility to the competition?

2. Leading Competitive Change
    - What changes should managers make to develop a competitive culture?
    - How are you going to build more leadership capability to bring about successful change?

3. Integrating Change into Operations
    - What should managers be doing to link competitive change to day-to-day operations?
    - What performance metrics are needed to track this integration?
    - What performance management measures should you be using?

4. Building Competitive Human Capital
    - How do you see learning being managed both individually and collectively at present?
    - What should managers be doing to improve both individual and collective learning?

5. Developing Competitive Agility
    - What do managers do to reshape and adjust strategies?
    - What should be done to manage strategic change and the emergence of threats and opportunities?

ACTION POINTS 4: FOCUSING CHANGE ON GAINING COMPETITIVE ADVANTAGE

Section 6: Is Your Organization Thriving or Just Surviving?

This section organizes contributors' comments to highlight what they see as the differences between *thriving organizations* and those that just get by—*surviving organizations*.

The first chart shows what contributors focus on when it comes to successful change.

Once again explicit references to customers and markets receive the least attention. Also, notice that in spite of 30 percent of contributors having difficulty with change metrics, measuring change is the category most commented on.

The next two charts summarize characteristics of thriving organizations and enabling and disabling factors.

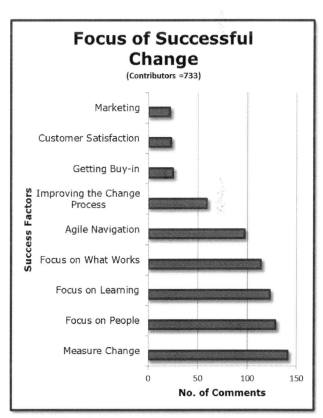

CHART 11: FOCUSING CHANGE TO WIN

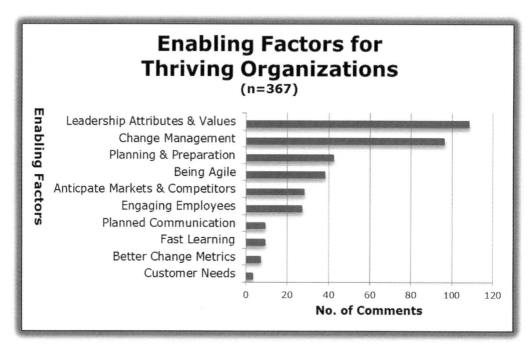

CHART 12: ENABLING FACTORS FOR THRIVING ORGANIZATIONS

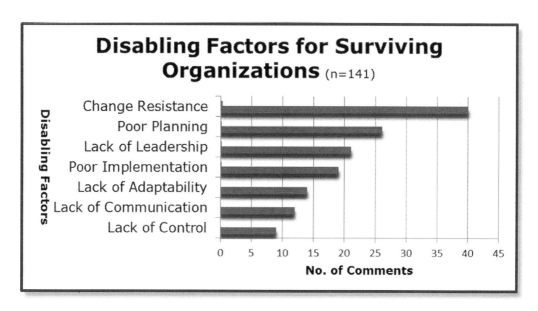

CHART 13: DISABLING FACTORS FOR SURVIVING ORGANIZATIONS

6.1. The Thriving Organization Assessment

As you go through this assessment, there are some things to bear in mind:

- This assessment is based on contributors' comments only. All we have done is organize them into a framework we hope is easy to understand.

- Not all assessments will strike you as relevant to your organization. So we encourage you to check those items that pique your curiosity concerning you and those in your organization of whom you're uncertain how they would rate themselves, their leadership, or your organization's current change initiative.

- *Technical Note*: Under each heading, you will see italicized contributors' comments to get a flavor of their *thriving or surviving factor*. In many cases factors are actual contributors' comments. Where there are no such comments, we have created a commonly understood or logical opposite (semantic differential).[11]

- This assessment is, as yet, untested; our intent is to validate these factors to create a robust and practical tool.

- This assessment's purpose is to facilitate leadership and change management teams' reaching agreement on where they need to focus to create a competitively vibrant organization.

If you want to be part of helping develop this tool, please give us feedback on which factors you choose and where improvement is needed to help other users. The assessment below is organized under the following headings:

1. **Leadership in Thriving Organizations**

2. **Change Management in Thriving Organizations**

3. **Planning to Thrive**

---

11 Semantic differentials are rating scales that measure commonly understood associations that some word or phrase carries. They are used to derive attitudes toward the given object, event, or concept.

4. **Thriving People**

5. **Communicating to Thrive**

6.2. Leadership in Thriving Organizations

There is an old saying: everything rises and falls on leadership. In your opinion, which of these attributes makes for a thriving or surviving company?

#	Thriving Leadership	Surviving Leadership	Relevant?
1	**Courage** Ability to look honestly and without ego at current state, and motivation to create future state desire to act courageously	**Lack of courage** Fear-based resistance to change Leading from the top down	
2	**Independent** Knows what they stand for	**Lack of leadership** Usually at the CEO level	
3	**Confident** Has done a full analysis of what the options are for improvement changes and how to implement them	**Lack of urgency** Just implement and then try to fix the problems during or after the change.	
4	**Risk-taker** Manage risk to take advantage and gain momentum	**Reactive** Lets change drive them Less likely to seize critical opportunities that may have not been present before	

#	Thriving Leadership	Surviving Leadership	Rele-vant?
5	**Trusting and trusted** Mutual trust and shared responsibility	**Top-down approach** Lack of consultation Authoritative not participative	
6	**Adaptable** Pays attention to changes in the environment, and when they adapt, they adapt selectively by keeping what works and eliminating what doesn't	**Inflexible** "We've always done it this way." Doing business the same old way: "if it ain't broke, don't fix it."	
7	**Communication and drive** Injects their values into the organization	**Inconsistency** Sends mixed signals Does what's needed but doesn't buy into the implementation, so results are not solid	
8	**Challenging people to grow** Empowers others to achieve their potential	**Failure to recognize people's influence on change** Doesn't see that people make or break the change initiative not the change itself	
9	**Embracing change** Sees it as a positive challenge to grow Makes change a part of their long term strategy.	**Fighting change** Sees change negatively; doesn't anticipate and embrace change Just tries to maintain status quo	

#	Thriving Leadership	Surviving Leadership	Rele-vant?
10	**Change-ready** Sees change as business as usual and embraces it with open eyes	**Change-resistant** Strong senior manage-ment resistance to change trickles down to lower levels.	
11	**Strong culture of trust** High-trust firms can try, and sometimes fail, but always learn and move on.	**Have low trust** With low trust, people are not willing to try new ideas, as they fear blame or failure.	
12	**Honest assessor** No ego when address-ing what is not working and effectively employing what works	**Lack of business intelligence** Reading customers and markets incorrectly and implementing the wrong change	

TABLE 4: LEADERSHIP IN THRIVING ORGANIZATIONS

6.3. Change Management in Thriving Organizations

#	Thriving Leadership	Surviving Leadership	Relevant?
13	**Change-ready** Prepare to thrive not just to survive	**Change-resistant** Too big to change—changes take too long and cost too much.	
14	**Change management is routine** People expect continuous change and development. Knows exactly what is expected and is not be alarmed by it	**Change is difficult** Can't adapt to change easily Inward focus Can't look outside market conditions and the competition, and can't adapt Afraid to ask for clarity	
15	**Support for change** Strong support for change and guiding the employee through the change journey	**Lack of support** Not enough supervision and support for those affected by the changes	
16	**Committed** All parts of organization want to change. Personal pride in ownership Accepts and even embraces change as the new norm	**Lack of commitment** Insufficient engagement and support for change, so results will be mediocre	

#	Thriving Leadership	Surviving Leadership	Rele-vant?
17	**Meaningful purpose** They spend time "smelling the horizon" and antici-pating required change. Time for strategic thinking means they are ahead of the pack.	**Lack of Purpose** Lack of drive and follow-through—so they change for the sake of change rather than changing for a good reason.	
18	**Strong case for change** Biggest driver	**Uncertainty** Inadequate reaction—sur-viving requires sticking to the out-of-date plan.	
19	**Adaptable** Willing acceptance and participation. Engages employ-ees, change agents, stakeholders	**Frozen** Protocols are officially changed, measured, and basically drive staff crazy. Uncooperative employees with a bureaucratic mind-set...inflexible...focused on self-preservation	
20	**Motivating vision** Caring about the future Clear strategy	**Lack of strategy** Conservative stagnation	
21	**Open-minded and non-resistant for change** They listen to what the environment is telling them, and take action to satisfy market demand.	**Complacent** Happy to rest on their past successes and don't see leading indicators and other signs of change	

#	Thriving Leadership	Surviving Leadership	Rele-vant?
22	**Shared benefit** The benefits of the change are known before implementation and serve as motivators and assessment of progress.	**Lack of benefit** Failure to communicate the benefits behind the change, change for the wrong reasons.	
23	**High tolerance for ambiguity** They are able to tolerate failure, and to look into the rudimentary causes of the failure and apply the lessons learned.	**Low tolerance for ambiguity** Finds change or the nature of business today frustrating.	
24	**Everyone aligned** Aligned	**Not even in the same book!** Not see change as an opportunity	
25	**Design for change** Change leadership engages the employees in the change and takes the time to gain their buy-in and participation.	**Imposed change** It's just forced from on high. It's more difficult and resistant Insufficient engagement	
26	**Control Change** Gain acceptance of your methodology Involve stakeholders Select quality change agents	**Lack of control** Failure to measure the before and after Lets change happen instead of meeting it head-on	

#	Thriving Leadership	Surviving Leadership	Rele-vant?
27	**Proactive, decisive, and focused** Being smart...taking steps quickly to reduce emotional pain of overall process.	**Lack of accountability** No consequences for not embracing the change	
28	**Assesses capacity to change** How much change can the firm and individuals take?	**No sense of the capacity to change** "We all can only cope with so much." Not enough change-management skills	

TABLE 5: CHANGE MANAGEMENT IN THRIVING ORGANIZATIONS

6.4. Planning to Thrive

#	Thriving Leadership	Surviving Leadership	Relevant?
29	**Understand your culture *first*!** Understand your organization's culture before embarking on the change journey. (Kotter & Slessinger)	**Doesn't realize the time it takes** Doesn't take time to think creatively and strategically.	
30	**Identify change requirements** Clearly define your vision and match with desired outcomes, well before the outcome is attained.	**Unclear goals** Fails to identify the desired results Change not prioritized	
31	**Prepares people for change** From top management to lowest level must be prepared for change and accept it.	**Lacks people preparation** Doesn't effectively anticipate the inevitable resistance	
32	**Market awareness** Understanding where/when change is required, planning, operationalization... Just do it rather than wait nervously to implement.	**Lack of market awareness** No sense of changing market conditions due to insufficient research data, so slow reactive actions	
33	**Anticipation** Deals with change by taking people on the journey.	**Lack of anticipation** Bad resource management	

TABLE 6: PLANNING TO THRIVE

6.5. Having the Agility to Thrive

#	Thriving with Agility	Surviving with Inflexibility	Rele-vant?
34	**Fast to change** Speed, timing, pace of change	**Slow to change** Change resistance is embedded.	
35	**Anticipates** Looks over the curve and sees things before they happen; no knee-jerk reactions	**Backward-looking** Impedes innovation	
36	**Flexible** Ability and will to change and adapt Speculating and preparing for change in advance of what the change is to impact	**Inflexible** Doesn't spot the need until too late	
37	**Willing to change with the times** Change to meet market and environmental threats. Changes continually in response to the changing needs of the market through change management and innovation	**Unwilling to ask the question** In what situations are your current strategies not working; are you being blown around like a leaf? You control change, or change controls you.	

#	Thriving with Agility	Surviving with Inflexibility	Rele-vant?
38	**Adaptability to changes** Planning...decision-making Evolves in the face of constant and often unpredictable factors Dictates how to cope with change	**React and respond** Rather than innovate, create and produce.	
39	**Responsive** Responds to external changes and decides our prosperity Evaluates where shortcuts can be taken (evaluating their risk on the way).	**Unresponsive** Doesn't recognize external changes that require internal change.	
40	**Flat organization structures** Better-working environment for every individual	**Traditional management structures** Poor organization structure	

TABLE 7: HAVING THE AGILITY TO THRIVE

6.6. Thriving People

#	Thriving with People	Surviving with People	Rele-vant?
41	**Trusting leaders** Treat them well, they tend to excel. Knows and believes in relationships based on trust.	**Distrusting leaders** Treat them poorly, they leave or give up. With low trust, people are not willing to try new ideas as they fear blame/failure.	
42	**Having talent and skill to implement** Being employee-driven really sets the company up for success. Those with imagination thrive.	**Lacking talent and skill to implement** Do not tap into their employees enough to help conduct planned change	
43	**Rewarding and recognizing** Incentive system Failure cannot be punished if valid efforts are made!	**Not recognizing or rewarding** Rewards for improvement are missing. Does not tie employee incentives to strategic goals	
44	**The toward state** Change allows openness, positive feelings about the future, optimism, and creativity.	**The away state** Change creates a large amount of fear, uncertainty, and lack of relatedness and fairness.	
45	**Motivated** Aware of the need to change	**Demotivated** Unaware of the need to change	

#	Thriving with People	Surviving with People	Rele-vant?
46	**Reaching their potential** Feel their true job potential has been reached; have support and a sense of worth	**Not reaching their true potential** Feel that their true job potential has not been reached	

TABLE 8: THRIVING PEOPLE

6.7. Communicating to Thrive

#	Thriving with Communication	Surviving with Communication	Rele-vant?
47	**Planned change communication** Making the employees comfortable with the change. Making the employees comfortable with the change.	**Lack of Transparency** In the change process... [employees are] not well communicated or educated about the change.	
48	**Constant and consistent** Throughout the process... Two-way engagement Build exceptionally strong relationships Respected communication	**Unclear, limited, and delayed** Lack of efficient and ineffective communication The communication style around change leads to change fatigue rather than creating an opportunity for staff to find the "what's in it for me."	

#	Thriving with Communication	Surviving with Communication	Relevant?
49	**Prepare information materials** About the coming change	**No materials prepared** Just receive change message as a rumor	
50	**Stakeholder communication** During all stages of the process	**Lack of stakeholder communication** Not helping people understand their roles and what they can achieve	
51	**Two-way engagement** Feedbacks and questions of the employees should be properly entertained to their satisfaction.	**No open lines**	
52	**Overcome or reduce fear** Don't create any more uncertainty than absolutely necessary	**Creates fear** Inconsistent and incomplete communication	
53	**Selling WIIFM (What's In It For Me)** The needs and benefits of a change initiative	No given change rationale No reasons and results	

TABLE 9: COMMUNICATING TO THRIVE

6.8. Learning to Thrive

#	Thriving Learning	Surviving Learning	Rele-vant?
54	**Encouragement** Right staff to improve commercial skills Constantly discovering, building, and growing through innovation	**Lack of encouragement** If the employee is not conscious about how she is perceived by others, she will continue believing in her own perception.	
55	**Belief in training and development** Build a learning organization...Training will give them the needed skills to be flexible and adaptable to new strategies.	**Lack of training and development** Worry about learning cost	
56	**Risk-taking** Being innovative and failing fast. Willing to take risks	**No risk-taking** Just sit back and watch the competition zoom past them and also take their staff with them	
57	**Learns from failure** Look into causes of the failure and understand and apply the lessons learned Follow-through is important, to give everyone feedback on the successes or failures.	**Blames others for failure**	

6.9. Other Thriving Factors

#	Thriving Customer Relationships	Surviving Customer Relationships	Rele-vant?
58	**Customer retention** Have a good product and strong customer relationship networks that they understand and stay in touch with	**Poor customer retention**	
59	**Customer satisfaction** Identify what the customer needs before even the customer realizes it exists Are sensitive to customer needs, delivering to customer what they promise	**Dissatisfaction with services/product**	
60	**Monitoring and measuring change** Focus of results	**Lack of control** Failure to measure the before and after	
61	**Uses dashboards** Integrated toolsets for current status	**Uses conventional reporting** Manual week-old, month-old, or longer reports	
62	**Accountability** They are empowered and accountable to the new process.	**Lack of accountability** No consequence for not embracing the change Not enough supervision and holding accountable by senior people who get stonewalled by old guard	

TABLE 10: OTHER THRIVING FACTORS

6.10. Action Points 5: Developing the Thriving Organization

This in-depth analysis shows the wide range of factors that go into developing the thriving organization. Our intent in being comprehensive is deliberate. There are no simple solutions or grizzly seven steps to follow. What we encourage is open debate in change-leadership teams to reach a broad and deep commitment of those few things that can make a difference between being ahead and just playing catch-up.

Action Points 5: Developing the Thriving Organization

Based on your answers to the questionnaire above, use the following questions to develop your plan for developing a more vibrant and competitive organization.

1. **Leadership in Thriving Organizations**
   - **What is the one thing you can do to improve your leaders focus for your current change?**
   - **What is your strategy for building leadership capacity and competence in the longer term?**

2. **Change Management in Thriving Organizations**
   - **Which aspects of change management do you need to address now?**
   - **What are you going to do differently in managing change in the longer term?**

3. **Planning to Thrive**
   - **How can you improve planning for change for the next time?**

4. **Thriving People**
   - **In terms of the current change, what can you do to focus people on making this change successful?**
   - **What is your focus going to be in improving peoples change readiness and agility?**

5. **Communicating to Thrive**
   - **Where do you need to focus in terms of improving communication?**

ACTION POINTS 5: DEVELOPING THE THRIVING ORGANIZATION

Section 7: How Effectively Are You Communicating Change?

In this section, contributors' comments are organized into the following parts:

- Methods of Communicating Change

- The Zone of Concern

- Poor Communication and Leaders

- Preparing the Ground for Change

- Putting the Change Team Together

- Communicating and Implementing Change—The Planning Process

  ➢ Analyze the impact of change

  ➢ Set up change program with measures

  ➢ Workshops and training

  ➢ Ongoing communication

  ➢ Implement and measure

- Outcomes of Successfully Communicated Change

7.1. Methods of Communicating Change

7.1.1. Introduction

The following analysis is based on 684 of the 1072 contributors who chose to add comments to their ratings on communicating change. This high level of participation reflects the challenges of rapid and accelerating change. Two pieces of evidence underscore the challenge many contributors face.

1. Their organizations go through a change every twelve months, or less often.

2. The need for each change is triggered by at least three simultaneous factors.

Here are two charts that illustrate why effective change communication is even more important to implanting change successfully.

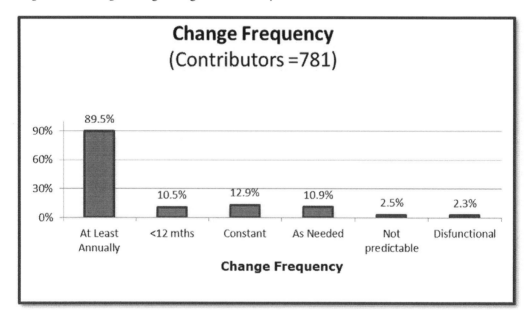

CHART 14: CHANGE FREQUENCY

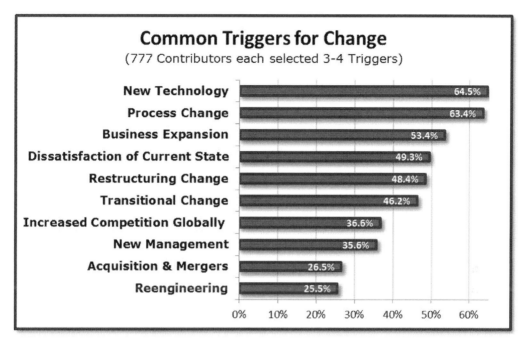

CHART 15: COMMON TRIGGERS FOR CHANGE

Of all aspects surveyed, contributors see this area as pivotal to change success. Part of their reasoning is that since 1996 surveys show the same change failure rates. Consistently, the one reason for failure cited by those executives surveyed was *people*. Curious, we wonder how many of those executives would agree with the benefits of better people management. Contributors noted the following:

- Greater employee satisfaction, which leads to more efficient production and better quality. In turn this leads to customers receiving more than what they are used to from other providers.

- Greater empowerment, which translates to greater agility.

- Greater morale, as people see themselves as part of an organization that is changing for the better.

- Greater awareness of change and employees' ability to respond more effectively.

- More people acting as ambassadors and marketers.

- More confidence to recognizing customer needs and possibilities to fulfill those needs.

Contributors to this survey see people at the heart of any successful change process. They see gaining stakeholder commitment as creating a forced multiplier of powerful change ambassadors. Essential to creating that commitment are leaders taking their people into their confidence and giving the reasons for change with honesty and courage. Our analysis also sheds light on some of the blind spots. For example, the chart below shows that 60 percent of contributors chose to make comments, and that the highest percentage of comments was regarding personal communication (24 percent), and poor communication was ranked third (10.2 percent). The chart below underscores contributors' focus and concerns.

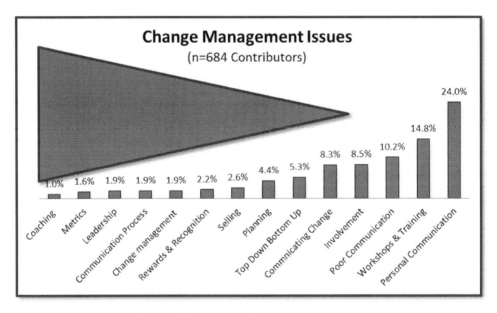

CHART 16: CHANGE-MANAGEMENT ISSUES

7.2. The Zone of Concern

As you will see, contributors focus on more on technique than systemic or strategic issues. Here is our commentary on the Zone of Concern.

Coaching and mentoring (1.0 percent) is the lowest ranked area, we think that this is understated and to some extent included in personal communication (24 percent). But it does not take away the lack of specific references to structured coaching and our concerns of why change fails. Contributors are not commenting on the role of the business coach in a change initiative. Here's The Worldwide Association of Business Coaches definition (adapted): a business coach underscores the specific focus and nature of coaching and why it should be a change imperative.

Business coaching is the process of regular, structured conversations with an individual or team. The goal is to develop awareness and behavior so as to achieve business change objectives for both for themselves, the change initiative, and their organization.

Such coaching enables people to understand their role in successful change and develop skills that are measurable and sustainable. The coaching process may take different forms, but throughout there is a clear focus on change initiatives objectives.

The business coach helps clients discover how changing or accommodating personal characteristics and perspectives can affect both personal and business processes. Successful coaching helps the client achieve agreed-upon business outcomes as an individual or team within the context of a change initiative. Business coaching establishes an atmosphere of mutual trust, respect, safety, challenge, and accountability to motivate both people coached and the coach.

Our concerns center on change success being predicated on individuals changing their behavior. Such changes are only achieved through frequency and intensity within a *requiring environment* of measurement, accountability, consequences, and rewards.

Change metrics (1.6 percent)—Here are comments from Section 4. They say,

- If you don't measure, nothing gets done…that is where it ends;

  ➢ You will never know if it worked or got results you like or intended;

  ➢ You can't manage what you don't measure;

  ➢ You have no idea of its success or failure;

- You can't determine effectiveness;

- You will stop making progress;

- You won't know if the change was needed at all;

- You will waste time and scrap it too late; and

- Management will continue to believe it was a success and then damage morale.

Overall many contributors commented on the consequences of not measuring change progress and results. Change strategies need observing and managing to assess their effectiveness. Such results can then be shared with employees, so they can learn and use. The key for these contributors is that

- Making performance visible is valuable for increasing change success, be it productivity, profitability, performance, or morale.

This marked lack of focus on developing metrics for measuring change progress is worrying. We know that more leading indicators (KPIs) are needed when a change relies on people to implement it.

Leadership (1.9 percent)— The lack of specific reference to *leadership* communication is puzzling, given contributors' references to poor leadership elsewhere in the report. Yet, successful change rests on leaders:

- Getting others to willingly follow.

- Being at every level of the organization.

- Having a clear vision, a vivid picture of where to go, as well as a firm grasp on what success looks like and how to achieve it. But it's not enough to have a vision; leaders must also share it and act upon it. Jack Welch, former chairman and CEO of General Electric Co., said, "Good business leaders create a vision, articulate the vision, passionately own the vision and relentlessly drive it to completion."[12]

---

12 Leadership Communication: A Communication Approach for Senior-Level Managers by Deborah J. Barrett, Rice University, Houston, Texas) 2006

- Communicating their vision in terms that cause followers to buy into it. Doing so requires clarity and passion, as passion is contagious.

- Continually doing something in pursuit of the vision, inspiring others to do the same.

Change Management and Communication Process (1.9 percent)— Communication about change management becomes even more complex when leaders and managers have to think about how best to communicate to all internal and external stakeholders. Any good communication plan depends on having a strategy, but as the audiences become larger, the communication strategy becomes more complicated. So we ask; Where is change communication's organizing framework? It seems glossed over or neglected.

Rewards and Recognition (2.2 percent)—*You get what you pay for* and *No money, no change.* So what rewards do people get for changing needs embedded in change communication? It's well known that stakeholders will resist change when they do not see any rewards. (See references to WIIFM.) Throughout this survey and in this section, no one is answering the question, Where are the rewards for people implementing change? Without rewards, there is no support for sustainable change. We see little reference to altering reward systems to support change.

Selling the Change (2.6 percent)—Few commented on the importance of selling the change as an essential element, although many would agree with this. We conclude that if leaders believe change is best implemented from top down, selling change is at best an afterthought. Yet here is the rub. So many contributors speak to the need for mutual trust and respect and the resistance to change when they are absent. There is an apparent disconnect between the predominance of one-way communication methods used by contributors' organizations—convenience is no recipe for commitment.

Planning (4.4 percent)—While many comments on the planning process were thoughtful and in line with many survey findings, the low level of commentary poses a question: Why?

One pervading theme of change communication follows:

- [Leaders] lack the ability to motivate or hold people accountable…They do a poor job at this…lots of saying nothing…People are told, not asked.

- Mixed messages occur often; leaders don't make [the message] about people… if at all.

- My company does communicate on change but it does little to measure the effectiveness of that communication.

So, the Zone of Concern is based on the low percentages in key communicating change areas. They seem to correlate with contributors' comments on poor communication and leadership, see what you think.

7.3. Poor Communication and Leaders

Our concerns deepened when analyzing poor communication, leadership, and resistance to change comments. Some comments read like a litany of limited, delayed, inconsistent and unclear communication with poor leaders who don't communicate how a change will work or be implemented.

For many contributors depleted and absent communication accounts for a major reason why people do not adapt well. They say, "No wonder change fails, and no wonder more change fails when people experience poorly implemented change."

For these contributors, leaders do not prepare their people for change especially how it will affect them. They allow the rumor mill to grind out a FUD flour.

7.3.1. They Don't Communicate

A third of contributors comment that they either didn't know of any change-related communication or that their leaders don't communicate enough or well. Here are some examples:

- I am new to my organization but have seen very little communication around change.

- No distinguishable process.

- They are poor communicators, [which] causes added stress.

- They have no consistent methods. Often it was up to departments and/or managers to establish and maintain methods.

They send an e-mail—and let the people make the change

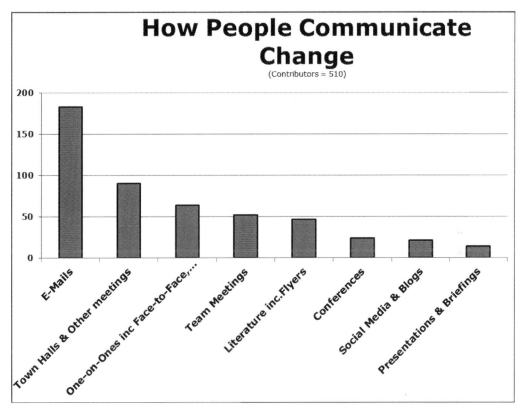

CHART 17: HOW PEOPLE COMMUNICATE CHANGE

This chart confirms that convenience and efficiency is the default forms of communication rather than those that are effective

7.3.2. Poor Leadership
Clearly all these commentaries of poorly planned and executed change lead inevitably back to a lack of sound leadership. Many comments refer to leaders' unwillingness to change—and when they do, it is from a protective or elitist position. People are consequently disempowered *and* disengaged from change.

Other telling commentaries on leader's contribution to failed change include:

- They don't change or communicate.

- [Communication about change is] very authoritarian and hierarchical.

- Most of the time, the management wants to stick to its ideology...although the business environment has already changed.

- They kicked the CEO out, which was not communicated to the people for a long time.

- My organization is run like a bully runs a playground. Lots of intimidation and fear and serves to perpetuate the division between people and executives.

- Truly, this organization is old school. Leaders protect their empire, and change rarely comes.

- Most change-related data is kept within the senior leadership.

- Ownership is not distributed and therefore not embraced by the people...It tends to be rumors heard through the grapevine.

7.3.3. Little or Poor Planning

- Mostly it is a last-minute effort after all critical decisions have been taken. No thought given on how to involve people in change. As one contributor said:

- Most organizations I have worked with do not notify the people soon enough and does not fully support the change and teams implementing the change. This creates conflicts among the stakeholders of this change process.

Other contributors' comments regarding planning include the following:

- In my opinion, my company doesn't effectively address those areas above [regarding planning] well enough to prepare people for change.

- Very little except advanced policy notices of change.

- Have no specific change strategy, which I think they should have.

- Don't prepare very well or none, no strategy and no people for change. Just rumors that things are going to change. No communication about how the change will affect people.

- Don't [plan]. It is inherent to our business culture. People involved are used to the dynamics of continuous change.

  ➢ A virtual command and control approach to change at present.

  ➢ Still, I am working with my organization on this issue; they are not ready for it. I believe change fails because they don't anticipate and manage the inevitable resistance associated with change.

7.3.4. Poorly integrated Training and Performance Management

Some responses indicate that training is used as *the change* with little consideration given how to implement what is learned. Here are some examples:

- My client organization only really does this through training workshops toward the end of the change life cycle, despite advice otherwise.

- They audit to ensure people are trained in the change; however, these audits are mishandled and are not really capturing the results of the entire staff.

- This was not done corporately; it was left to individual staff—some did, and some didn't. The company did spend a lot of money on our training and education as a senior team, though. (We all had to get MBA's to progress and all had team-building programs too.)

Essentially, a major reason for failed change is when poor communication increases fear, uncertainty, and doubt. These feelings are the core of change resistance. These emotions are ignored at your peril if your change effort is to stand a chance of building people's commitment, openness, and willingness to change.

Also, lack of faith in management is directly related to increased employee *anger, frustration,* and *anxiety* with regard to the change. Once distrust is created, cynicism then takes root. What follows is a slide into negative relationships, little commitment, poor job satisfaction, and ultimately change failure.

We now turn from the Zone of Concern regarding poor leadership and communication to look at what these experienced change managers say is needed to increase your chances of planning and implementing successful change.

7.4. Preparing the Ground for Change

This part covers how contributors seem to focus on getting their organizations ready for change before they plan, communicate, and implement a specific change. They cover the following areas:

- Top-down vs. bottom-up change

- Advocacy for top-down or cascaded change

- What about a different approach—Bottom up?

- Involvement

- What do we stand for?—Gaining agreement of change communication values

- Getting people change-ready

- Change agents

- Stakeholder involvement

Many researchers show that real change requires authentic communication and dialogue across all organizational levels. Although employees' resistance and disagreement is unavoidable, it can be managed through multiplexed and constant communication. As one contributor commented,

To achieve such change, change communication has to center on *establishing and retaining trusting relationships*. If employees feel fairness and consideration, they will trust more. Trust is the glue of success.

> **"If people do not change,**
>
> **there is no organizational change."**

- We found that trust in management was the only variable that significantly impacted the emotions of change resistance.

- Trust is very often the outcome of people's sense of justice—feeling [there is] fairness, the quality of supervisory communication, and their own self-esteem… People's self-esteem is the degree to which individuals believe they are capable, significant, and worthy.

The challenge for change managers is that the timing, involvement, and sequence of communication either helps or detracts from people's sense of fairness; namely,

- How organizational decisions are applied to different groups,

- How the procedures are developed and used, and

- How people are treated individually.

7.4.1 What Is Communication's Role in Reducing Change Mistrust?

Our analysis yields the following overarching factors of communication are needed if people are to feel enabled:

- Two way, multilevel, and cross functional

- Focused on addressing people's emotions and feelings

- Focused on transparent transmissions of the objective reasons for change

- Using a multiplex of media

Contributors stress that creating trust is never an overnight success. Many recognize that it's not an accident that transparency, trust, and a purpose-driven culture exist. Such cultures are created only through purposeful leadership that does the following:

- Shares their vision

- Adapts how to get there based on people's input

- Believes in engaging people to embrace all aspects of change

- Builds through careful recruitment, selection, and development

- At its core is the role leaders play in:

- Understanding the psychological process people go through in first letting go then understanding the new destination and how they can get there

- Convincing people to leave home

- Facilitating a culture of change

- Consistently showing the way forward—sometimes routinely, sometimes inspirationally, and where the exchange is mutual and meaningful

As one person put it,

- As the top person in your business, others look to you for direction, not only in terms of business needs, but also related to behavior, ethics, and standards. If you want others in your business to change, you must set an example for them to follow. You need to provide sufficient support for your people via leaner structures, greater resilience, and better empowerment.

Several recognize that big changes occur due to external factors, which are often unexpected. For them it is an ongoing practice and part of their world. The focus is getting ready for the inevitable. These contributors' suggestions make the point that you should make every effort *in advance* of starting a change:

- Success depends on anticipating change…invest in quality staff and outcome.

- Teaching and leading their people to be change agents

- Practicing everyday creativity skills

- Proactively developing problem-solving and decision-making skills

- Continually working on your communication skills

- Developing individual and team skills that are scalable under pressure

The more you can create an agile, change-embracing organization, the greater your chances of thriving while others struggle. So when change hits, you can respond with less stress and fear.

Others stress the balance of not being all things to all people. Knowing what you stand for is a counterweight to deciding when to flex people's agility. Contributors cite their long-term purpose: to guide their response to new opportunities. They stress ensuring that this purpose is well understood and that people see they link between their personal and the organization's purpose.

This leads to focusing on ensuring people

- Know exactly how they can help and

- Are placed in work that matches them well.

This is an integral part of a clearly defined and accepted change process. It's also a key part in being agile and having people committed to the change process.

For these contributors, it's about laying the ground work for their people to *embrace constant change responsively.*

Part of getting any organization change-ready is ensuring that the leadership team is clear on the trade-offs and blending of top-down and bottom-up driven change. This clarity of leadership is is best conducted before any specific change is considered, as it takes time to implement changes in leadership and management style: for example, recruiting different management styles so that square pegs fit in square holes.

We conclude that this survey's findings send mixed messages on how to implement change successfully. A simple example is that while many advocate consultative change and involving people in decision-making, contributors say they still seem to use one-way communication methods (e.g., e-mail).

So here's the debate between these two leadership styles and what contributors said:

7.4.2. Top-Down, Bottom-Up Change

A top-down approach to change management implies imposed change as the initiative comes from the top. Decision-making is centralized at higher levels of the firm, excluding lower-level people in the change process, even though they are directly affected. Top-down change is about making changes quickly and dealing with the problems only if necessary. The problem is that top-down approaches to change management increase resistance—the biggest problem in changing any organization. Regardless of how well these top-level decisions are made, change management will be insufficient, because leaders ignore so much of the organization. Where the leader makes all the decisions and expects subordinates to follow, this creates resistance to change. Naturally people's first reaction to imposed change is resistance.

Change based on unidirectional and traditional approaches has definite limitations. As contributors point out, this approach rests too often on leaders clinging to the belief that power, privilege, and success lie in their core group.

7.4.3. Advocacy for Top-Down or Cascaded Change

From senior managers, and then through line managers, down to individuals with communication is a model being led by business leaders at various levels of the organization. Broadcast through line management, and give good reason for change adopted. Contributors also stress the following:

- Leaders need to own the change initiative.

- Leadership commitment to the change is crucial.

- Top management demonstrates their support.

- Integrate change into day-to-day operations.

For those contributors advocating a top-down approach, the most common term is *Cascaded Communication*. They recommend using a leadership-briefing cascade. Many make references to such tactics as the following:

- Team calls and one-on-one conversations

- Accountability for communicating the change and ensuring it is applied

- Leading by example—directly and personally

- Communication using process descriptions and the Internet, including webinars.

Change based on unidirectional and traditional approaches has definite limitations. Problems usually cited include the following:

1. Decision-making is limited to the top of the organization; therefore, a lack of information, suggestions, and ideas coming from the bottom.

2. People at the top are not willing to listen to lower-level people' ideas, suggestions, or feedback, resulting in poor employee motivation and performance.

3. There is very little task delegation involved in the change process, thus lower-level people can feel they are somehow incompetent and underqualified for such tasks.

4. Keeping the change process to the upper level of the organization breeds skepticism among the lower-level people.

5. Misunderstandings occur because of communication problems and inadequate information of both parties.

6. Many differing assessments to a given situation exist in lower levels and different functions. Lower-level people don't know for sure the exact circumstances revolving around the change and thus resist it.

- Team model of communication through managers

137

7.4.4. What About a Different Approach—Bottom Up?

Bottom-up change management traditionally seeks to involve those affected in the process of change. It seeks to avoid the pitfalls of imposed change by allowing individuals within their working groups to come to terms with change. Bottom-up is often associated with an emergent change process such as trends in technology that demand rethinking. What markets do we want to play in? And with what technology?

This approach typically runs into several problems, being too slow to respond effectively to short-term business demands. When change comes from the grass roots of an organization, it takes a considerable amount of time to diffuse the change throughout the organization, particularly to the higher-ups. In essence, this approach is based on collective decision-making.

Here's what some contributors commented:

- Changes are always started in a company meeting, then on to smaller team meetings, so that everyone is part of the process. Change is built ground-up, bottom-up, and at every…opportunity as we conduct our daily activities.

- We don't communicate change; we invite our people to help us initiate the change.

- We involve people in dialogue…a million times better than to "download" from above.

- Continuing upper-management-to-employee communication regarding changes, and continued employee satisfaction.

- Direct communication to employee from top management personal appearances.

Many contributors comment that the tension between top-down or bottom-up change is highlighted by the question of involvement.

7.4.5. Involvement

The debate over developing genuine involvement, where people's ideas are considered and used, comes up against those who seem to pay lip service to this issue. Here's an example of the fine line between involvement and manipulation:

Manipulation

- If I have an idea that I would like them to buy into, I suggest it, gather several of their responses during the ensuing conversation, then reiterate their ideas back to them, integrated with mine in such a way that it appears as though they had come up with the original idea. Then I give them lots of praise for thinking of it!

Genuine Involvement

- I am very careful to remember that these people all have significant expertise in their own fields (they are all the talent), so when they offer a suggestion, I always listen carefully and consider it. Usually they turn out to be right, and we're [all] glad that they came forth, because we all take pride in a superior product or result.

These two contributors' examples underscore the fine line between good intentions and sending mixed signals. Intentionality both in the values held and how they are communicated is crucial to many contributors. Here's a chart of the comments on communication intent.

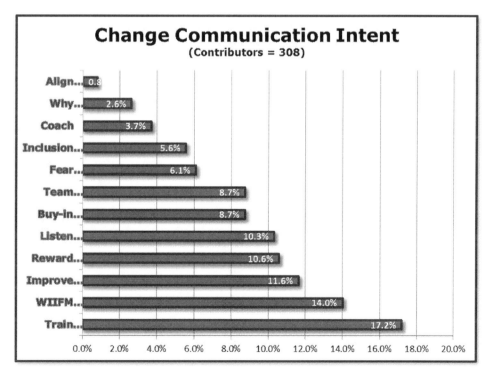

CHART 18: CHANGE COMMUNICATION INTENT

These comments were included in this analysis if they indicated the purpose or intent of their change communication. Some points to draw attention to are the following:

- Throughout, contributors rarely mention getting people *aligned* or use any similar phrase. Yet it is interesting that, regarding all aspects of disabling factors mentioned in section 6 and its references to the causes of resistance, we infer that getting people on the same page is crucial to change success.

- Sadly, explicit references to coaching remain sparse. Yet change is so dependent on modifying people's behavior, so they can stop doing things that are counter to the change's goals and starting doing things that ensure its success.

- Note the larger proportion of comments related to selling change as in WIIFM[13] (14 percent), buy-in (8.7 percent) and inclusion (5.6 percent)—a total of 28.3 percent.

- The reference to fear means to allay fears (6.1 percent).

- Lastly we see much contributor focus is on training. You may say, What's the problem with that? The problem is the lack of focus to ensure training has any impact. For example, there are too few comments on setting expectations, coaching, performance management, and measurement and rewards. All these elements are needed to change behavior and part of the requiring environment.

The next table poses more questions. How likely it is that leader could be misinterpreted?

Change Management Communication Content (Contributors =281)	Percentage
Change Process Change/Change Management/ Process	**38.1%**
Strategy Vision/Purpose/Desired Outcome/Future/Mission/ Objectives/Goals	**17.8%**

13 WIIFM = What's In It For Me

Change Management Communication Content (Contributors =281)	Percentage
Measure Metric/KPI/Dashboard/Budget/Review/Appraisal/Assessment/Surveys/Milestone/monitoring/LEAN/Performance	**13.9%**
Plan Manageable Chunks/Pros and Cons/Research	**13.5%**
Culture Living/Meritocracy/Innovation/Creativity	**9.3%**
Customer Market/Competitors/Trial of New Models	**6.4%**
Other Selection/Succession Planning/Governance	**0.7%**

TABLE 11: CHANGE MANAGEMENT COMMUNICATION CONTENT

7.4.6. Summary
Many leaders pull out their hair and say things such as the following:

- Why don't they get it!

- How many times do we have to tell them that!

They are exhibiting the familiar signs of misalignment with their people. These data give an insight why they could be misinterpreted and mistrusted. Here's a snapshot of the last three data sets:

1. Leaders are not focused on coaching, metrics, leadership, communication process, or rewards/recognition. This is our Zone of Concern.

2. Over half of the communication methods used are one-way (289 out of 510 comments).

3. The leader's intent does not seem to focus on the culture, roles, or governance. In fact, out of 755 comments, only 14 were about roles and responsibilities

Based on your own work experience, how would you feel in such a hypothetical environment? What is the likelihood that your trust in the leadership would erode?

Our analysis is that the more change leadership stays in the hands of the few, the more the many will feel stressed, resistant, or, at best, confused.

PICTURE 1: BEHAVIOR ICEBERG

For many, this data is like an iceberg. The rational side of change is the 10 percent that leaders present and tend to focus on, above the waterline. Meanwhile, below the waterline (90 percent), many are trying to relate the rationale for change with their own values, beliefs, needs, and past change experience. Such leadership communication patterns are not conducive to getting below the waterline and helping people reconcile organizational change with personal change. The result is often unnecessary stress, resistance, and confusion.

That leads us to advocate what our contributors are saying in laying the groundwork for successful change. The first criterion is developing a shared governing set of values and then getting people ready for the inevitable change ahead.

7.4.6. What Do We Stand For? Agreeing on Change Communication Values

For many, *people values* are at the core of effective communication. Essentially, *treat people as you want to be treated.*

Here's what people say about genuine involvement:

- Transparency is key; otherwise, people will have reason to doubt and mistrust the initiative and therefore find ways and means to deliberately undermine the process.

- Taking care of the human element and their attendant emotions.

- Effective change needs:

  ◦ Trust

  ◦ A compelling logic

  ◦ A close match of leaders' actions and words

  ◦ A commitment of those who are affected

  ◦ Respect for people (even departing)

- Build a culture in which change is for the larger benefit of the organization and not for an individual getting affected positively or negatively.

Contributors Comments on Genuine Involvement

- **Making every employee part of the change-management process from the start to keeping them in the loop**
- **Involving people from start to finish in strategy development and planning**
- **Asking for contributions and understanding people's issues as well as helping them find their own solutions…letting people choose which ones to become involved in, or assign change projects based on their input**
- **Listening to their needs and goals while inviting collaboration in the process. Continuous involvement in the organization strategic goals**
- **Engaging people in co-designing the change process**
- **Engaging people in decisions that affect them, so that they get the issues and [feel] some ownership**

7.4.7. Getting People Ready for Change

Here's a sampling of how some leaders get their people change-ready:

- Train in market and socio-economic factors, then get [your people] involved in generating ideas to improve the situation.

- Ensure all people understand the organization's core values, purpose, and vision to guide us. Clarify strategic objectives and engage people in problem-solving.

1. Demonstrate how they build on the results they like and reverse-engineer the results they don't.

- Banish blame from the culture through leveraging high levels of transparent communication.

- **Giving people responsibility they can manage, and allow them to do their job with clear expectations and regular reporting**
- **[Encouraging that] people tell us what needs to change and...working with them to implement**
- **[Initiating changes] at employee level. During the change process, communicating progress. Everyone bought in, has a voice, a perspective, and is tied to the outcome.**
- **Individually...listening to concerns and acting**
- **Shared progressive improvement and encourage involvement recognizing opportunities for change**

- Listen to their ideas and seriously consider them.

- Regularly meet to discuss vision and strategy, so people are familiar with the organization's room for maneuvering.

- Build esprit de corps by helping people to feel part of the whole process, and give recognition that change is largely in their hands.

- Ensure they know their part in planning the next change.

- Develop common spiritual and philosophical concepts underpinning the change cross functionally to develop the engagement process that will be responsible for changing the work culture for good.

The next stage in getting ready for change is selecting and developing specific change roles.

7.4.8. Change Agents

While a few contributors cite using a proprietary change management model—like, Prosci, Adkar, and Kotter—a few cite introducing external change agents. Far more make reference to selecting internal change agents and engaging stakeholders to lead the charge. Additionally a few advocate setting up a central organizational development and design group.

- We first advise staff of the changes that we [are] thinking of making and what, if any, input they would like to share that we might have missed or overlooked. Progress begins the idea of change for them, so when it happens, it's not a surprise but already a realization in their minds.

7.4.9. Stakeholder Involvement

Some of the earliest activity for these contributors is the involvement of stakeholders and change agents. This starts with stakeholder analysis:

- Assign ownership to each process, then document and communicate the changes to the stakeholders.

- Identify and engage change agents up and down the chain to communicate and mentor people.

- Establish the change organization, and communicate who is responsible for each activity.

- Ensure that roles and responsibilities are rational.

- Identify change agents and conduct pre- and post-meeting and interacting with stakeholders.

- Introduce directly applicable tools, methods, and ideas.

- The organization publishes policy and establishes governance for the elements of the change. These measures establish responsibility for the change but fall short of creating a sense of ownership.

7.5. Putting the Change Team Together

Several contributors advocate putting a change team together before a specific change is planned or started, so that a team is part of laying the foundation for successful change:

1. Appoint a Change Manager who is sponsored by the most powerful stakeholder. Their role is to engage leadership and team members in projects when their scope is identified then to do the following:

- Gain their input

- Develop their buy-in

- Continually engage them

- Get the business to sign off

2. Appoint a Change-Management Team to establish change-management metrics, reporting, and documentation. Then do the following:

- Decide how this information is shared during weekly meetings to keep up-to-date.

- Decide how this information is shared with the rest of the company.

3. Select And Appoint Champions From Stakeholders And Change Agents who will be responsible to cascade and implement the change before planning is too far advanced. Only select those people that fulfill the criteria below:

- Demonstrate adaptability

- Tolerate high degree of ambiguity

- See the need for change and can communicate it

- Demonstrate great emotional intelligence

- Relish the responsibility and authority of implementing change

- Lead hands-on so they can

  ➢ Identify and involve enablers at all levels in the design and implementation to gain their commitment;

  ➢ Develop the messaging that conveys openness and honesty while giving full information; and

  ➢ Establish an atmosphere in which they can express their fears and needs and take these into consideration.

4. Design a Change-Measurement Framework, because measuring progress runs the gamut from surveillance to reviewing personal satisfaction with regard to the policy, balance scorecard, and quality management system. The key is to decide your change measurement framework, ideally before planning a change's implementation and communication. Two contributors shared the following suggestions.

- We measure and report on change at every level and by every employee, and their contribution to the change increased the bottom line.

- Ensure change requirements are part of performance management.

- Publicize responsibilities and accountabilities and how they are integrated into their annual review and evaluation process, incorporating these measures and new requirements into the culture.

- Use surveys. They are critical to the change process, as management can easily acquire input and gain buy-in by reviewing personal satisfaction.

5. Communicate Through Workshops so that people have the opportunity to ask questions and build any necessary skills. Also make sure that they know in advance what are the expectations related to the change.

- Ensure that all management understand the change from top to bottom

- Get regular updates from employees to ensure that training objectives are met

- Ensure that current training matches the needs for change. The best way to do this is to ask employees the type of skills they need in order to implement change successfully.

So, having aligned the leadership team on

- The values they share about people,

- Getting the organization change-ready, and

- The cascade of change champions and enablers,

we are now ready to look at what our contributors say about the specifics of communicating change.

7.6. Communicating Change—The Planning Process

We are now into planning a specific change and what contributors suggest. The first step, often needed but often missed, is analyzing the specific impact of the envisaged change. This is important, as all change initiatives may be similar in many ways but crucially different in others.

This first step helps reduce assumptions and grounds planning in evidence rather than conjecture.

7.6.1. Analyze Change Impacts

Many contributors criticize those who launch a change without this preparatory step. They advocate analyzing the likely change impacts, such as the following:

- Identify the real reasons for change, and decide how to get this message heard by different groups.

- Start with a small pilot project. Let other people see how the change works.

- Refine the process from that experience before implementing in the rest of the organization.

- Assess the impact on the current reward system.

- Realistically estimate the time and effort for the change.

- Limit the number of top priorities.

- Identify how to deliver quick wins, such as internal surveys, to know how they are likely to respond to the change, and provide them with feedback.

- Consider the emotional challenge in change for all key individuals and departments, and proactively map a plan to minimize resistance based on emotional intelligence and the use of the emotion road map.

- Assess leaders, roles, and how they should model and coach.

7.6.2. Set Up Change Program with Measures

In this section we will take the results of the assessments above and similar assessments that contributors advocate. Contributors' comments are below:

- We include things through talking about what "is" looks like and they tell us how they will adopt it.

- We have champion groups, effective communication streams, and regular loops. Our people understand where we are heading and all change is related back to this. Then develop…clear definitions of why, how and where the change will take place.

- Develop positioning—why are we doing this? How are we going to do this? And what is in it for you and your organization?

- Communicate the direction being taken and the adjustments that will be needed.

- Ensuring that people understand where the business is heading.

- How it plans to get there.

- What will people be doing, what will people not be doing.

- What support people will get to make changes.

- Tailor the communication plan to each stakeholder group.

- Divide the change plan into multiple projects so that change is organized in manageable pieces.

- Explain what is expected of them and why.

- Ensure accountability and communication is defined, loud and clear.

- Get them involved in the change and make them a part of the new situation especially in decision making in relation to pros, cons, and why the management decided to go for it.

- Redrafting key responsibilities and KPIs on job description.

- Behavior change and what will be necessary.

- Problem solving strategies by letting them take ownership and responsibility for improvements.

- Taking their views from the planning process so that even they take the responsibility for change.

- Giving assurances that change will be with due respect to people (even those departing) and explaining well the why and how any restructuring requires. Planning for new roles or compensating for managing out

- Show your staff and volunteer leadership the value in change by benchmarking through test modules…Instill in them a sense of security so that they come to the change with open arms.

7.6.3. Workshops and Training

All employees from all disciplines are trained at how, who, when, what, and where to initiate a change. Use vehicles such as retreats and one-on-ones to get over exactly what is changing. Some contributors advocate the following:

- On-purpose programs and tools to grow the people and, in turn, grow the business

- By having the CEO continually teaching top-level and midlevel management

- Programs, effective communications, courses, studies and properly educating people in the advantages at the initial stages

As one contributor commented,

- We rely strongly on effective communication via multiple media. We strongly embrace and train our people to take advantage of the various forms of social media, the Internet, and interaction. We foster involvement by bringing in the majority of the people in the preplanning stage.

7.6.4. Ongoing Communication

Many contributors specify regular communication for constantly reinforcing and sustaining commitment and for adjusting plans from the feedback they get:

- The frequency is weekly updating and constant brainstorming.

- We meet as a team to discuss problems and opportunities, discuss options, choose the best ones, and develop…action plans, assign roles, and 'go.'

- Inform them in every step taken—with the why, what, where, and when.

- Keeping communication lines open.

- Continuous reinforcement and how change is linked to core purpose of company.

- Keeping in constant communication when adopting new procedures.

- Be available and approachable with questions.

- Keep them in the loop of what is happening and about to happen.

- Publicize and praise good behavior.

- Ongoing coaching and one on one coaching/conversations

- Regular two-way transparent communication with clear support from executives.

- Inform them what is happening (favorable or adverse).

- Check people's understanding of what's happening.

- Address areas of greatest concern. Concerns are always there so encourage the people to voice them and make it easier to move forward.

- Regular change conversations...Most managers understand the change, [but] they often have trouble applying it back to the business, so it is particularly important to tie it to the business.

- Most of all celebrating your successes regularly.

7.6.5. A Contributor Summary

Give people the long-term vision of where they ought to be, give them a road map on how to get there, structured mentoring, and coaching at regular checkpoints. Personal communication works better as people have an opportunity to interact with the initiator of change and to better understand it. This instills in people a sense of security, so that they welcome the change with open arms—to do this they suggest the following:

- Identifying and engaging change agents up and down the chain in the organization

- Continuously communicating the vision and what's in it for everyone

- Realistically estimating the cost and time for change

- Emphasizing role modeling and coaching

- Providing ongoing training and support

7.6.6. A Reflection on Change Communication

Contributor comments on change management values and communication planning include the following:

- The aim is to have as many open individual discussions with people possible. Then you can get a read on:

  ➢ What they would like to do;

  ➢ How they would like to do it;

  ➢ Greater ownership of training, development, and mentoring;

  ➢ Highlighting what achievement looks like and how it feels; and

  ➢ Helping each employee be aware of how he or she is perceived by others.

This sums up many comments on the values, purpose, and motivation behind communication during a change initiative. Open discussions with all information available and reasons why things will change are fair game. It's important to get buy-in and ownership. If they are missing, chances are the change will not become part of the company culture.

7.7. Outcomes of Successfully Communicated Change

For the reader, the following is a litmus test of healthy sustainable change. It's the outcomes many commentators are striving for; it's about helping people feel that

- They are trusted and can trust their leaders;

- They are valued;

- They can speak up;

- They are listened to;

- They own the change;

- They communicate change, not management;

- They are part of the company;

- They pride themselves in their company's competitive position; and

- They are needed.

More than ever, change leaders use a plethora of communication methods that are both easy to use and cheap, but here is the rub. Contributors speak repeatedly to individual communication that is respectful of a person's individuality. Communicate to individuals individually, is what they are saying. This is not to discount practical concerns such as speed and the need to deliver communication to all people at the same time. It is a cautionary message; as one person said, "If you can't make your deadline, *don't e-mail me, pick up the damn phone!*"

7.8. Conclusion

Overall, we found little explicit reference on issues that would seem crucial to improving people's alignment to a change. Issues such as change management, communication, and change measurement were referred to in less than 6 percent of the comments. These setup issues were worryingly low: concerns about the requiring environment or accountability

Where's the Change-Requiring Environment?

The requiring environment is a set of aligned change expectations between leaders and individuals.

These expectations flow in two directions. The first are the leader's expectations for each person in terms of activities and behaviors that they are to stop, start, and continue doing—the reciprocal being the expectations people have of their leaders.

When these are agreed upon, the requiring environment's foundation is set.

Change managers then build accountabilities, performance measurement, and management as well as rewards schemes to ensure expectations of both leaders and their people are met.

culture (e.g., coaching, rewards and leadership) were also under 6 percent of comments made.

As we looked in more detail, we saw that leaders were directly criticized. A third of comments said that our contributors either didn't know of any change-related communication or that their leaders didn't communicate enough or well. *They don't communicate!*

Below is a sampling of such criticism:

- Unwillingness to change, and when they do, it is from a protective or elitist position. People are consequently disempowered and disengaged from change.

- Mostly it is a last-minute effort after all critical decisions have been taken with no thought given on how to involve people in change.

For contributors, real change is the outcome of authentic communication. Contributors are clear that "dialogue" is not a fancy word for communicating. It's their conviction that *dialogue* is a conversation between groups and individuals, often in tense situations. Dialogue aims at a resolution through exchanging ideas and opinions. What contributors say is that although employee resistance and disagreement is unavoidable, it can be managed through multiplexed and constant communication; one contributor commented as follows:

"If people do not change, there is no organizational change."

> **If employees feel fairness and consideration, they will trust more, and trust is the glue of success.**

To achieve this communication requires focus on establishing and retaining trusting relationships. If employees sense fairness and consideration, they will trust more, and trust is the glue of success. Contributors often commented that trust in management was the only variable that significantly impacted change resistance.

Yet comments on authentic communication and building trust seem to collide with those related to top-down-led change. Critical contributors point out that top-down rests too often on leaders clinging to the belief that power, privilege, and success lie in their core group. Those who are more positive prefer to terms like cascaded communication and briefing cascades. Whatever blend of top-down and bottom-up approaches, it is clear: be intentional, and, as one contributor said,

- Being solid in the values you hold as a leader needs to be clearly articulated and solidified to your change management team before you start planning.

This is invaluable to avoid being misinterpreted and mistrusted. It's what our contributors are saying is key to laying the groundwork for successful change. The first criterion is developing a shared governing set of values and then getting people ready for the inevitable change ahead.

Once your leadership team has a solid commitment on *what they stand for,* then you can be really proactive and get people change-ready.

Some of the earliest activity for these contributors is the involvement of stakeholders and change agents. This starts with identifying and engaging change-agent stakeholders *up and down the chain to communicate and mentor people.*

This leads to several contributors putting the change-management team together *before* a specific change is started, to design the change.

A critical activity for the leadership team is to design the change-measurement framework. Only then we are ready to look at what contributors say about the specifics of communicating change. Many contributors specify regular communication for constantly reinforcing, sustaining commitment, and adjusting plans from the feedback they get.

7.9. Action Points 6: Implementing an Effective Change-Communication Process

The following questionnaire is based on 755 contributor comments on implementing an effective communication-change process. It is designed for those involved in change leadership to select relevant questions and reach a consensus on improvement areas.

Implementing Effective Change Communication					
Analyzing Change Impacts					
How Well Does Your Change Communication Rate?	**Not Well**			**Very Well**	
	1	2	3	4	5
ACI1 How well have you identified the real reasons for change?					
AC12 To what extent have you agreed on how to get this change message heard by different groups?					
ACI3 How much thought is given to piloting the change *before* implementing it across the organization?					
ACI4 How well have you assessed the impact of change on the current reward system?					
ACI5 To what extent have you got realistic time and effort estimates for the change?					
ACI6 How well have you planned for those involved in the change to carry out their normal duties?					
ACI7 To what extent has planning focused on delivering quick wins?					
ACI8 How well have you assessed the emotional challenges key individuals and departments will face?					

Implementing Effective Change Communication					
Analyzing Change Impacts					
How Well Does Your Change Communication Rate?	Not Well		Very Well		
	1	2	3	4	5
ACI9 How well are you planning to proactively reduce people's stress and resistance?					
ACI10 How well have your assessments of leaders, managers, and other stakeholder roles impacted how they should model and coach?					
Totals					

Implementing Effective Change Communication

Set-up Change Program with Metrics

	How Well Does Your Change Communication Rate?	Not Well			Very Well	
		1	2	3	4	5
CP1	What is the quality of planning in regard to talking people through the change and get their input on how to it?					
CP2	To what extent have you taken their views from the planning process and assigned responsibilities for change?					
CP3	How well have you set up champion groups, effective communication streams, and regular feedback loops?					
CP4	How well have you developed clear definitions of why, how, and where the change will take place? (Highlight the disadvantages for them to stay in their current situation: pros, cons, and why the management decided to go for it.)					
CP5	How well do you communicate mission and vision through consistent leadership messages, giving out the same message each and every time?					
CP6	To what extent have you got a broad commitment to closing gaps between the current and desired states?					

Implementing Effective Change Communication

Set-up Change Program with Metrics

How Well Does Your Change Communication Rate?		Not Well		Very Well		
		1	2	3	4	5
CP7	How well have you developed change positioning? (It should include the direction being taken and the adjustments that will be needed, as well as the concerns listed below: Why are we doing this? How are we going to do this? What is in it for individuals and our organization?)					
CP8	To what extent does your implementation plan include the following: What are your expectations? What will people be doing? What will people not be doing? What support people will get to help them make their own changes? What accountabilities and communication are needed?					
CP9	What attention has been given to redrafting key responsibilities, KPIs, and job descriptions?					

Implementing Effective Change Communication

Set-up Change Program with Metrics

How Well Does Your Change Communication Rate?	Not Well			Very Well	
	1	2	3	4	5
CP10 How well have you defined and explained the necessary behavior changes?					
CP11 How well have you tailored the communication plan to each stakeholder group?					
CP12 How well have you divided the change plan into manageable pieces?					
CP13 What are your problem-solving strategies for midcourse corrections that still allow people to retain ownership and responsibility for improvements?					
CP14 How well have you prepared to give assurances that change will be with due respect to people (even those departing)?					
CP15 How well have you planned for new roles or compensation for those you are managing out?					
Totals					

Implementing Effective Change Communication

Ongoing Communication and Training

How Well Does Your Change Communication Rate?		Not Well			Very Well	
		1	2	3	4	5
OGC1	How well have you developed your strategy to engage employees from all disciplines in training them how, with whom, when, to what purpose, and where to initiate a change?					
OGC2	What deliberate programs and tools have you to grow the capabilities and skills of your people and, in turn, grow the business?					
OGC3	What roles will executives, including the CEO, play in continually teaching top-level and midlevel managers?					
OGC4	What role will multiple media take to ensure effective communication (e.g., social media, Internet, and other interaction)?					
OGC5	How well have you planned for regular communication to inform people of every step taken, with the why, what, where, and when?					
OGC6	Do you meet together as a team to discuss problems and opportunities?					
OGC7	What ongoing coaching and one-on-one conversations are you planning?					

Implementing Effective Change Communication						
Ongoing Communication and Training						
How Well Does Your Change Communication Rate?		Not Well			Very Well	
		1	2	3	4	5
OGC8	How do you plan to keep communication lines open for listening, adapting to feedback, and talking to those who are stressed by the change?					
OGC9	How do you plan to recognize progress, celebrate individual success, and reward people?					
	Totals					

TABLE 12: CONTRIBUTORS' COMMENTS ON IMPLEMENTING
EFFECTIVE CHANGE-COMMUNICATION PROCESSES

Action Points 6: Implementing an Effective Change-Communication Process

Based on your answers to the questionnaire above, use the following questions to develop your plan for developing effective change communication.

- Have you established an explicit set of shared governing values?
- How are you getting people ready for the inevitable change?
- Have you engaged stakeholders and change agents?
- Have you put the change-management team together?
- How do plan to align the team's values of change and their expectations of one another?
- How are you going to improve leaders change communication skills?
- Who is going to ensure that real change will be the outcome of authentic communication?
- How are you going to ensure that all your people know and understand your change rationale?
- How are you going to monitor employee's sense of fairness and trust? (Remember: trust is the glue of success.)
- How are you going to establish dialogue between groups and individuals, in often tense situations?
- How are you going to establish and monitor your change's requiring environment? Is there a set of aligned change expectations between leaders and each individual?

ACTION POINTS 6: COMMUNICATING THE CHANGE REQUIRING ENVIRONMENT

Section 8: How Can You Lead to Thrive?

8.1 Reflections on Leadership

Clearly from this survey leadership skills that focus change to win are at a premium. Today, change is the norm. It is neither random nor regular but hovers somewhere in between. It is a condition of having many diverse yet interdependent components linked through dense interconnections. How these interrelationships arise and how they challenge organizations is not well understood (IBM & KMPG Surveys endorse see page 13)

It's time for a debate about how leaders can develop rewarding not just working relationships today. It is the competitive core – energizing people and harnessing technologies better than anyone else. The ultimate standard for such rewarding relationships is a leader's ability to sustain superior results over an extended period.

Why is this debate needed?

Unfortunately too many leaders are seen as self-serving. People have lost trust. They respond best to learning not "command & control". Most importantly, they are searching for genuine satisfaction and meaning. What we mean by leadership and leading needs to be redefined. Complexity is not going away – its exploding. Worryingly surveys show, for example:

- Only 40 percent of senior executives rated themselves as "very effective" manage complexity - What happened to the other 60 percent!

- Less than half believed their enterprises are ready for highly volatility and increasing complex environments.

Here are three aspects for leaders to consider:

165

Aligning: Sustaining superior performance relies on aligning people with their company's essence by distributing and empowering leaders at all levels. This is the most difficult task. Aligned employees who commit to that essence want to be part of something greater. For example: Johnson & Johnson's Credo is a classic that guides everyone's actions.

> "When expectations are articulated but ignored, an important part of the company's shared purpose is shut away. By contrast, when expectations are made a central part of the company's shared purpose, and put out in full view, they become like a beacon: a guiding light as to how to move toward a common goal. It becomes easier to speak honestly or to reveal information, when people know that this behavior is okay"
>
> (Based on Peter Senge's Fifth Discipline Fieldbook)

Empowering: Traditional leaders delegate limited amounts of power to keep control. We don't live in that environment anymore. In contrast, leaders need to empower all levels while ensuring commitments are met. We need empowered leaders who set standards for other employees.

Collaborating: Businesses today are too complex to foster a culture of individuality. Achieving lasting solutions needs collaboration that spans organizations, customers, suppliers, and even competitors. Leaders must foster collaborative spirit. Top-down leaders may make short-term results, but only the really authentic leaders can galvanize sustained long-term performance[14]. Organizations filled with aligned employees focused on serving customers will outperform traditional competitors every time.

8.2 Why should leaders focus on the essence of their organizations?

The Essence is an amalgam of mission, vision, values, intent and ethics. These components are the focus of aligning and realigning people, rather than delivering the corporate stone tablets down from Mount Sinai (or wherever the senior management strategic planning retreat was held).

---

14   Adapted from Bill George's perspective of Aligning, Empowering and Collaborating. Bill is Professor of Management, Harvard Business School and former CEO of Medtronic

Sustaining an organization's essence is a dynamic that require everyone's engagement to define, reaffirm, refine and redefine as needed under changing situations. And don't let that word "everyone" slip you by this is an organizationally deep process.

It's only by leaders "inter-reacting" that they can develop people's shared clarity about the organization's essence – "what we stand for!" From shared clarity comes confidence, from confidence comes cohesion and from cohesion comes the freedom to decide and act. That's how organizations will stay on track today. Many people making many decisions true to their organization's essence.

In Section 7, there is strong evidence that leaders interact but not "inter-react" Why is it an important distinction in terms of leading in complexity? It takes raises attention above the bland to a richer form of communication - "inter-reacting" Its communication which is neither top-down or bottom-up.

Think of each person as a neuron in their "Organization's Brain" and the lines of expectations with others as synaptic connections. One way expectations are weak synaptic connections until they are agreed and committed to by another neuron. You need an expectation alignment process like AlEx™[15] that facilitates and measures the creation of aligned expectations so the "Organization Brain" grows and learns to handle complex change. It becomes effectively self-diagnosing, exposing unnecessary tasks or lack of resources. So, as each neuron fires its sets in train a whole series of inter-connections and reactions. There is continual feedback and reaction that builds agility.

8.3 What are the dangers of using technology to increase control?

Technology increases the illusion of greater control which can feed leader's "Control Addiction". More measurement equals more control. But measuring what is easy to measure can have the very opposite effect. The problem is that most of what is easy to measure has already happened. What is difficult is forecasting what is likely to happen. We can't spend more time looking through the "rear view mirror" when we have a winding road ahead of us. Technology's cheapness and speed feeds this addiction by access to evermore data and information at the cost of acquiring knowledge and wisdom. As[16] Charlene Li wrote.

---

15 Aligning People for Greater Success, The Crispian Advantage - http://wp.me/PNJ0z-jY
16 Open Leadeship, Charlene Li, 2010 Josse-Bass

> "…let's face it information leakage is everywhere, your company missteps spreading over all the internet to all your customers, business partners and employees….an even if you don't want their opinions they will be out there."
>
> "The question isn't whether you will be transparent, authentic and real but, how much will you let go and be open in the face of new technologies. Transparency, authenticity and …being real are the by-products of being open"
>
> (Open Leadership by Charlene Li)

This means that shared clarity and therefore aligning people will be ever more difficult to set up and sustain, especially if people don't know what their organization stands for.

This problem magnifies when there is no coherent place for technology in your firm's strategy. So, technology's attraction is a leader's distraction. It detracts from:

> "Leadership is a relationship between those who aspire to lead and those who choose to follow"
>
> (The Leadership Challenge by Kouzes & Posner)

This relationship becomes critical as organizational structures flatten, fueled by more knowledge working. It's not about leaders taking more control but "loosening the reins". The more leaders let go, then reciprocal relationships and the power of self-control can grow. We are not short of examples of moving toward self-management. For example, Gore-Tex, Whole Foods, Google etc.

> "…having the confidence & humility to give up the need to be in control while inspiring commitment from people to accomplish goals"
>
> (Charlene Li – Open Leadership)

Today, a paradigm shift is underway fueled by social technology and rapid change. Clearly this is not easy to achieve.

8.4 Why do we have difficulty developing leaders that can thrive in today's conditions?

Today's conditions are not good proving grounds for the leaders we need. More of doing more with less, multi-tasking and the growing doubt that we may be doing the wrong things means that decision-making, and expectations are now more compressed. Section 1's findings underscore this condition. Under such compression, leaders can lose the ability to stand back and assimilate.

Consequently, entrenched expediency leads us into solving one problem so quickly that we find we have now created five more problems. We are so busy trying to solve problems there's no time for "Where the hell are we going?" These conditions are not good for selecting or developing leaders who can work well under fluid and complex conditions.

What's happening to leader and follower relationships in such turbulence? Imagine the impact on a fear-based command and control culture. Subordinate leaders are just "waiting for the other shoe to drop"[17] and the blame game to start:

The Blame Game

Everybody was sure Somebody would do it. Anybody could have done it, but Nobody did it. Somebody got angry about that because it was Everybody's job. Everybody thought Anybody could do it, but Nobody realized that Everybody wouldn't do it. It ended that Everybody blamed Somebody.

Reinforced, of course, when the guilty are promoted and the innocent hung.

---

17 "waiting for the other shoe to drop" is defined as awaiting a seemingly inevitable event, especially one that is not desirable

8.5 What can I do about leading in complexity?

Ask yourself:

- How much of my needs to control are bound up with my own insecurities and ego?

- How much control do I really need to produce the right outcomes?

- How well do I really engage those I lead? (If you think this is the same as participation, you are wrong!)

- How well aligned are my people with the Organization's Essence and where it's headed?

Your answers gauge just how reciprocal your relationships really are, and the extent of shared clarity about your organization's essence.

The key is "inter-reaction" when teams who are closest to the "coal face" can openly discuss success and failure. The purpose is to take lessons learned and use them to repeat success and avoid failure. Such outcomes are the foundation of "inter-reaction" that ultimately creates rewarding relationships.

Benefits of Inter-reaction

- Understanding more clearly original intent, what thought processes drove decisions, what outcomes resulted, their real and likely consequences. So, as much attention is devoted to the "Why" as the "What". (See Section 1)

- Developing better solutions because of understanding the reasoning used. So, future mistakes will decrease.

- Reporting outcomes of such reviews to make recommendations that increase others learning. So, avoiding mistakes and capitalizing on successes.

- Embedding regular open communication and knowledge-sharing nurtures strengths and remedies shortcomings that improve morale,

- Building distributed leadership and growing the next leader generation

Above all, inter-reaction creates the synergies needed to develop best-of breed customer value and most of all great people. Successful inter-reaction ensures the team produces greater impact than individuals could do on their own. Here's an example:

The Benefits of Inter-Reaction – An Example

During the Korean War, Col. John Boyd, USAF observed that the North Koreans had better jet fighters. But, what he did notice was that US pilots had superior skills. He concluded that pilots were too focused on overcoming their technical inferiority rather using their superior combat skills. So, he came up with the idea. "What if we can make faster decisions than the enemy? After all, we already have the ability to execute better than they do". He came up with a fast cycling decision-making process:

- **Observe**
- **Orient**
- **Decide**
- **Act……Rapidly**

He concluded decision-making is the result of rational behavior in which problems are a cycle of Observation, Orientation (situational awareness), Decision and Action. This loop (OODA Loop) enabled US fighter pilots to succeed in combat because they increased their decision-making speed which meant they outmaneuvered and confused opposing pilots. It is now used by the U.S. Marines and other organizations.

Such shared cycles help people stand back from their emotions, objectify problems and make people's thought processes transparent. This is crucial to distributing leadership. Without this transparency leaders can't see how to coach effectively and can only work if there is shared clarity on the essence of what the organization stands for. Such tools need to be embedded into an organization's relational fabric.

A Final Thought

Leader's greatest impact is when they motivate their followers to action by appealing to their shared sense of essence - what is important and worth doing well. This occurs when leaders engage in ways that enable their followers to higher levels of motivation and morality to the point of common purpose.

Our position is that it's only by energizing people and harnessing technologies better than anyone else that organizations can survive and thrive. Genuinely aligned, empowered and collaborative people will outperform the competition every time. A leader's role is to create successful change that fulfills people and avoids human casualties. Leaders need to create working relationships that are rewarding not just superficially productive.

Unfortunately, this survey shows, in Section 7 especially, that when the urgent drives out the important, many leaders ignore what their "guts" are telling them, even when they sense people aren't on the same page. They've sensed it before and seen the results. Yet, complexity and urgency mask how things accumulate, misalign and make each change more difficult. You know that feeling yourself. We've all worked in dysfunctional work places. You pick up on people's differences and how they use their experience to justify their positions. They are oblivious of others views. Worse still, they believe that their views are shared by everyone.

If leaders are aware of these things, why don't they do something? We think it's like how people put up with pain and stress - take more pills and go on. Here are some examples of what leaders ignore and don't realize their effect:

- It's expecting things to be done and repeatedly being disappointed. It is the lump in the stomach when handed yet another impossible deadline.

- It's feeling that they have to be a mind-reader to figure out what is expected.

- It's that welling anger they get when important decisions fall apart (because there really wasn't any buy-in).

These are all misalignments of people not being on the same page. It's costly, pervasive and accumulates.

Now, add increasing complexity and we need to say – we can't go on like this anymore. The busy-ness of complexity masks misalignments especially when wicked problems get into the mix.

Wicked Problem Solving

Horst Rittel coined the term "Wicked Problems" as he found traditional approaches to design and planning were only effective for solving benign or simple problems. For example:

- Gather data

- Analyze data

- Formulate Solution

- Implement Solution

This apparently very reasonable approach starts faltering when:

1. You don't understand the problem until you have developed a solution.

You can't search for information without having some sense of what a solution looks like. And what 'the Problem' is depends on who you ask – different stakeholders have different views about what the problem is and what constitutes an acceptable solution.

2. You don't have a nice neat ending.

If there is no defined 'Problem', there can't be a definitive 'Solution.' So you can't solve the problem with the 'correct' solution. Herb Simon, called this 'satisfying' -- stopping when you have a solution that is 'good enough'

3. You don't have right or wrong solutions.

Solutions are simply 'better,' 'worse,' 'good enough,' or 'not good enough.' How "good" they are will vary widely and depend on different stakeholder values and goals.

4. You can't draw on past experience

There are so many factors and conditions that no two wicked problems are alike.

The point is managing complex and wicked problems shifts the center of gravity toward peoples' relationships and interactions. It shifts from relying on expertise and pride in accumulating knowledge to learning with and from fellow learners, honestly disclosing doubts and admitting ignorance.

The implications for Focusing Change to Win is that complexity and misalignment are best handled by those directly involved. So, leadership should be devolved to the lowest level. This means that leading learning is a core competence that needs urgent improvement to be a bastion against the confusion of poorly managed complexity.

Leading Learning

Leaders have to shed their prejudices of bad experiences of learning at school and that learning by doing is good enough. Many leaders will have to unlearn, and re-learn about leading learning

Ask yourself:

- What expectations do we have of people to develop shared knowledge from similar situations?

- How well are you set up to use shared situations to build common frames of reference?

- How much effort have you put into enabling people to express feelings of being puzzled or being misunderstood?

- How clear have you been that making sense of problems and developing solutions needs to be through reaching understanding, resolving differences and producing an agreed course of action?

- How well have leaders, especially senior leaders, consistently expressed their expectations of learning to all levels across the organization?

8.6 The benefits of leading learning and Focusing Change to Win

- Knowledge and reasoning need to be used for collective sense-making.

- Positive shared experiences strengthen organizational culture.

- Shared situations builds shared learning and reduces the exclusivity of individual experience

- Sharing puzzlement develops learner ownership because there's "gas in their tank" to do something about it.

- Getting people on the same page only happens when people's feelings are transparent to others. It takes the guesswork of where people are coming from. It reduces assumptions about people's intention, motivation and agenda

- Stakeholder and team member interests of are more likely to be respected and served

- Better alignment leads to growing trust and openness which leads to people being less guarded

- A social process that bonds people together. As we engage with others we influence and are influenced by our working community their beliefs and values. This type of participation is how we absorb and grow a healthy culture.

This is how we grow as individuals and develop rewarding relationships. So, leader's expectations need to shift from the individual to the team. It is the blending of people, their experiences, values and beliefs that are not reducible to individual actions in complex situations. Information isn't any good if it is not shared in ways that others can understand. If leaders don't insist and lead others to interact with each other then the chances of building trust, respect and other relational glue is remote. It is therefore imperative that leaders:

1. Hire people who evidence lifelong learning – if people aren't curious they are not for you.

2. Make sure you pay people for doing different things not just doing what we have always done - if you don't you will get what you've always gotten.

3. Ensure that all people know learning is a priority and it's not something left to chance or the competition.8.7

8.7 Action Points 7: Leading to Thrive

Action Points 7: Leading to Thrive

A Leader's greatest impact is when they motivate their followers to action by appealing to their shared sense of their organization's essence. Use these questions to rate your leaders abilities:

- To what extent do your leaders focuse on developing rewarding not just working relationships?
- How reliant are your leaders on "command and control"?
- How well do they really engage those they lead?
- How well do they foster a culture of collaboration? Consider both internally and externally.

Leading to the Essence

Do your people know what your organization stands for? Specifically:

- How well understood is the organization's essence? (mission, values, intent and ethics)
- How well aligned are my people with the Organization's Essence and where it's headed?
- To what extent do leaders use the essence to guide and coach their people?

Developing Leaders
- To what extent are you distributing and empowering leaders at all levels.
- What evidence do see of true "inter-reaction" where success and failure are openly discussed?
- To what extent do they then take lessons learned and use them to repeat success and avoid failure.
- How well do they use processes to help people stand back, objectify problems and make people's thought processes transparent?
- To what extent does the urgent drive out the important and mask how things accumulate, misalign and make each subsequent more difficult?

Problem Solving
- How often do your leaders try to solve complex problems with processes geared to "benign or simple problems"?
- How often do leaders face complex or wicked problems?

Leading Learning
- What expectations do we have of people to develop shared knowledge from similar situations?
- How much effort have you put into helping people express being puzzled or misunderstood?
- How well do they lead people on tackling problems and solutions by sharing understandings, resolving differences and producing an agreed courses of action?
- How well have leaders, especially senior leaders, consistently expressed their expectations of learning to all levels across the organization?

ACTION POINTS 7: LEADING TO THRIVE

Appendix 1

Focusing Change To Win
Leadership Change Manual

Appendix 2. Contributor Demographics

A2.1. Contributor Countries

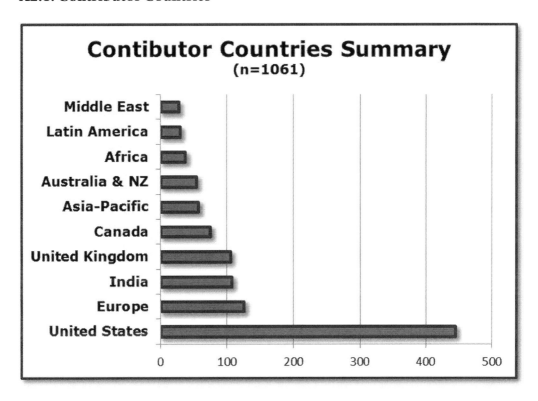

A2.3. Industry Sectors

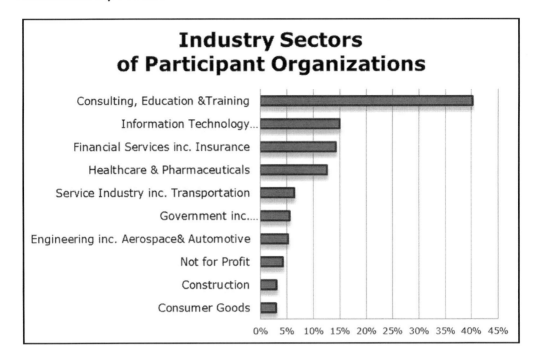

A2.3. Contributor Job Titles

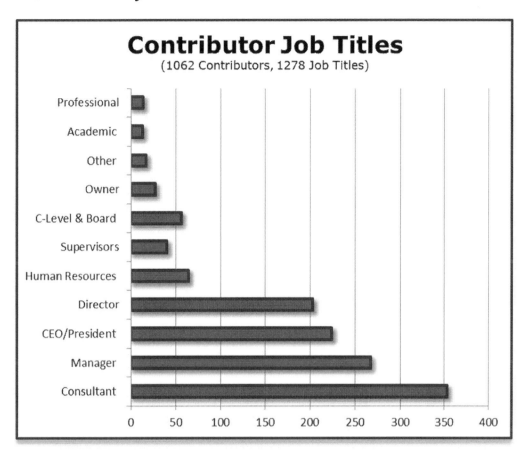

A2.3. Number of Employees per Survey Organization

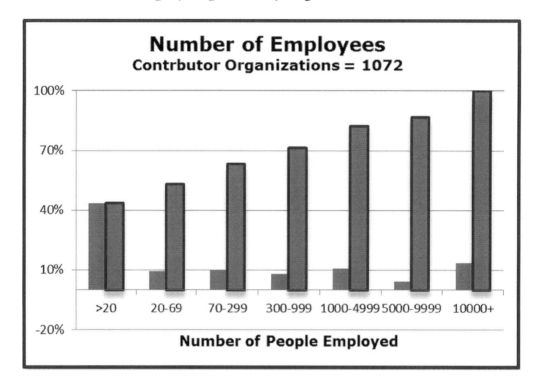

Appendix 3. Charts

A3.1. How Often Does Your Organization Initiate Change?

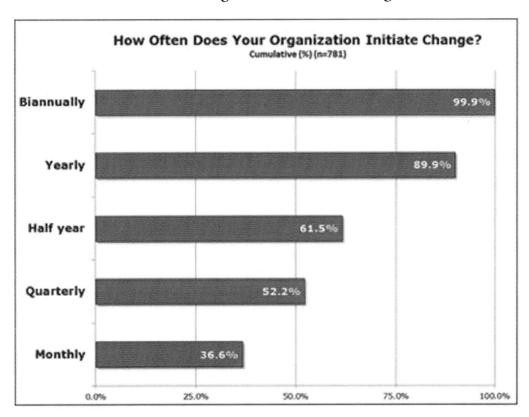

A3.2. Common Triggers for Change

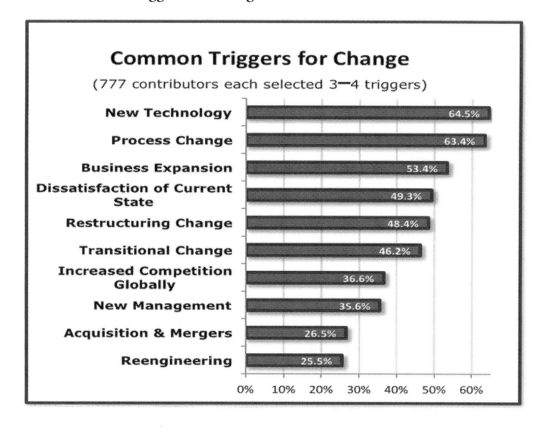

A3.3. Do You Measure Change Effectiveness?

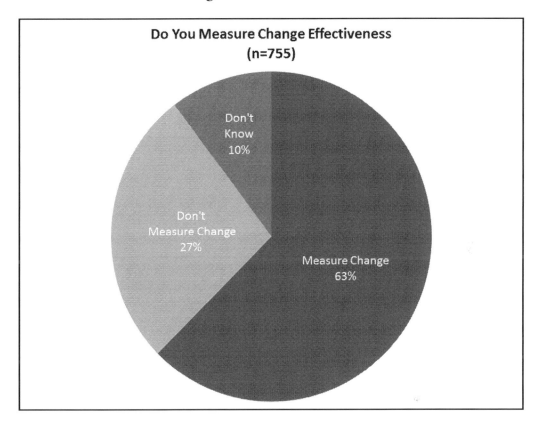

A3.4. How Well Do You Measure Change-Management Processes?

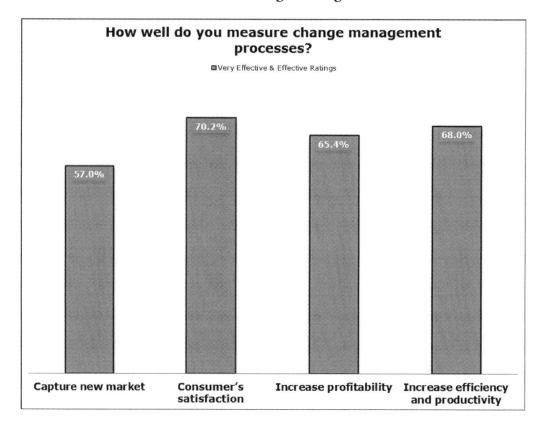

A3.5. Benefits of Measuring Change

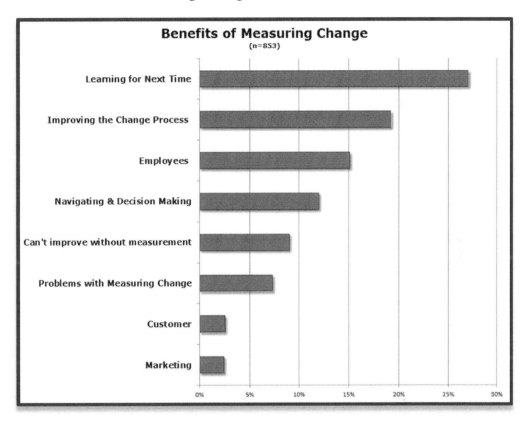

A3.6. How People Communicate Change

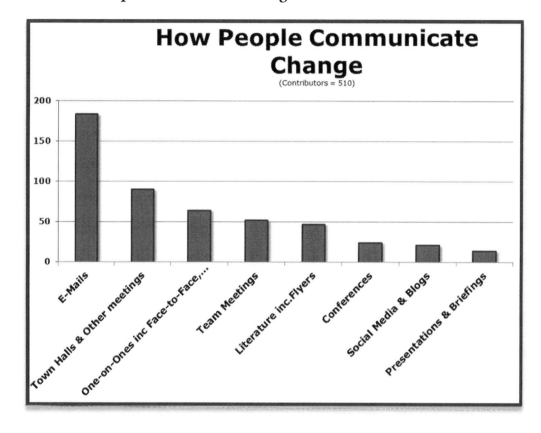

A3.7. Employee Metrics

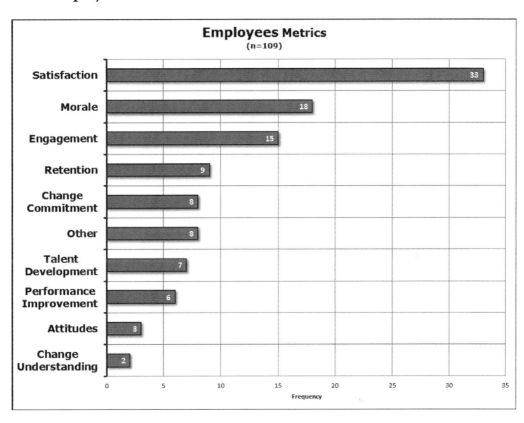

A3.8. Gaining and Retaining Competitive Advantage

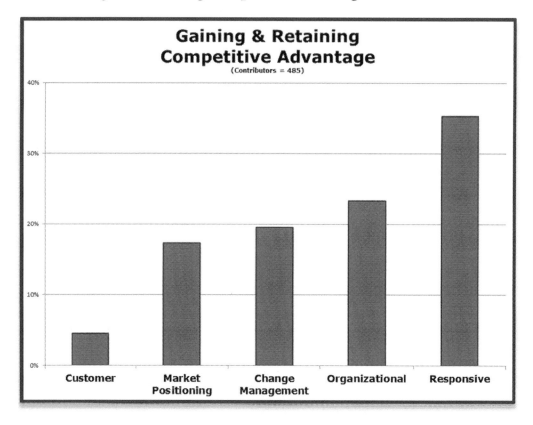

A3.9. Focus of Successful Change

A3.10. Enabling Factors for Thriving Organizations

A3.11. Disabling Factors for Surviving Organizations

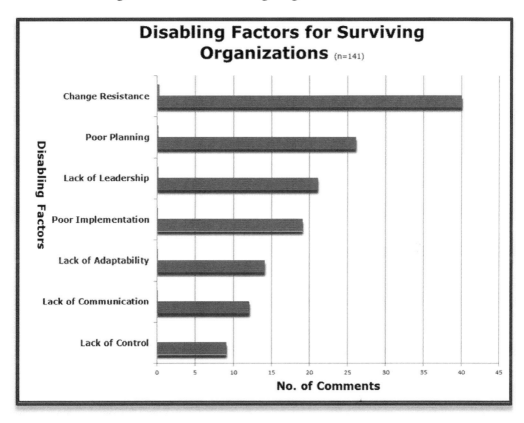

A3.12. Change Frequency

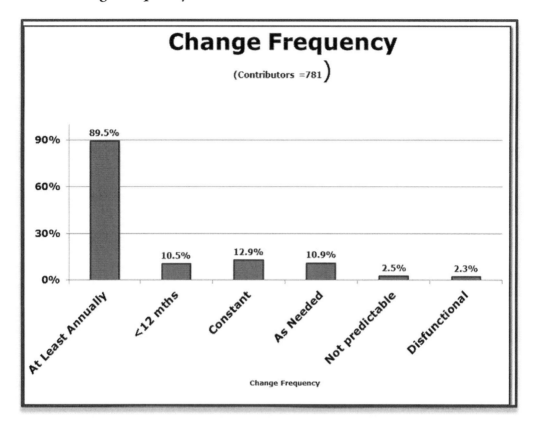

A3.13. Change Management Issues

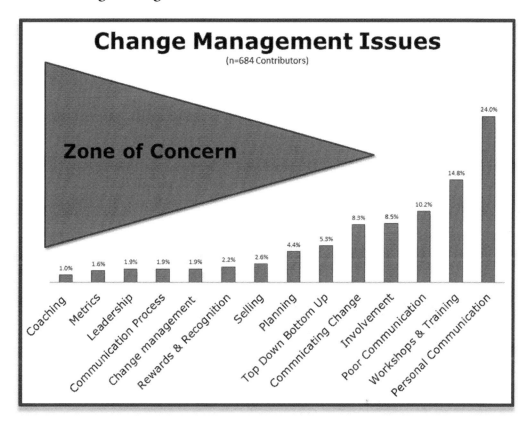

A3.14. How People Communicate Change

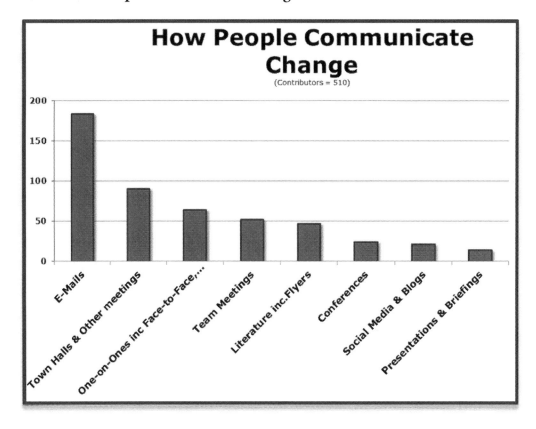

A3.15. Change Communication Intent

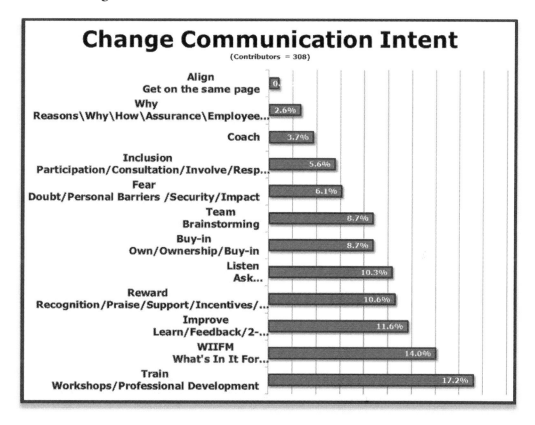

A3.15. Most Common Reasons for Losing Customers

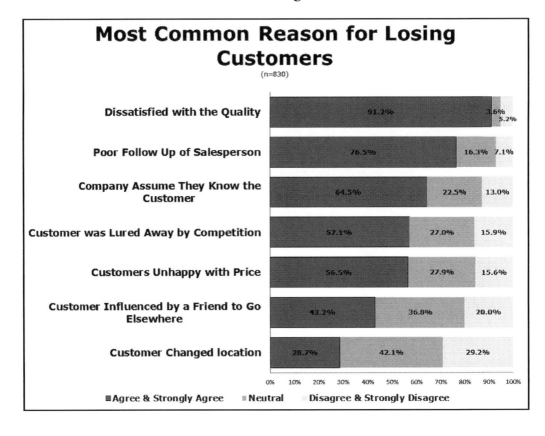

A3.16. Resistance to Change Factors

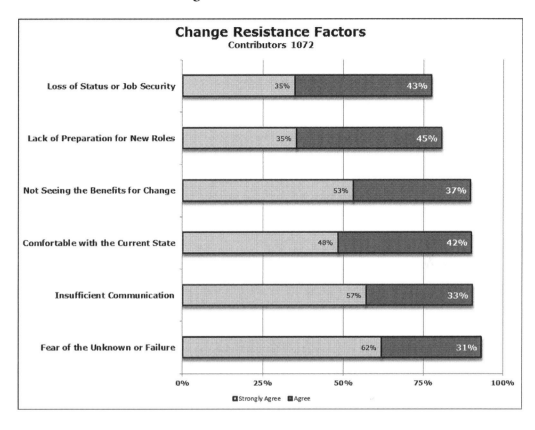

Change Resistance Factors
Contributors 1072

Factor	Strongly Agree	Agree
Loss of Status or Job Security	35%	43%
Lack of Preparation for New Roles	35%	45%
Not Seeing the Benefits for Change	53%	37%
Comfortable with the Current State	48%	42%
Insufficient Communication	57%	33%
Fear of the Unknown or Failure	62%	31%

◨ Strongly Agree ▨ Agree

About the Authors

Kelly Nwosu is the managing consultant of New Catalyst Management Services. He obtained his BSc from Coventry University, UK, and Diploma in Business Administration from University of Abuja. After leading research projects on change management and leadership with more than one thousand professionals in over nineteen industry sectors representing eighty countries, he has gained extensive international experience required to deliver sustainable change. This research examined the challenges faced by business leaders, senior managers, HR leaders, and other professionals while planning and leading change programs. He provides consulting, training, and strategic tools that could be widely used by organizations to manage the human side of change, improve performance, and ultimately achieve success.

Nick Anderson is principal of the Crispian Advantage. He has extensive experience in managing and leading effective change. After leading behavioral research, productivity, and change management projects over thirty years, he has a deep understanding of what it takes to lead major human capital projects that produce valued results. These projects span process improvement, behavioral research, and change management across software, hardware, manufacturing, retail, and professional service. Nick has worked with GlaxoSmithKline, Royal Bank, Hewlett Packard, First Telecommunications, IBM, Digital Computers, Sun Microsystems, London Stock Exchange, EDS, and Global Access Point. He has a masters in human resource development, with distinction, from Nottingham Trent University. He is also a fellow of the Chartered Institute of Personnel Development and a chartered management consultant.

For more information about this book

To give feedback, arrange a speaking engagement, or discuss how we may help your organization, you can reach us by any of the following means:

Book site: www.focusingchangetowin.com

Official site: www.newcatalyst.net

E-mail: info@newcatalyst.net

Made in the USA
Charleston, SC
11 October 2014